SIGNING THE SCRIPTURES

YEAR A

A Starting Point
for Interpreting
the Sunday Readings
for the Deaf

Joan Blake

LITURGY
TRAINING
PUBLICATIONS

SIGNING THE SCRIPTURES: A STARTING POINT FOR
INTERPRETING THE SUNDAY READINGS FOR THE DEAF,
YEAR A © 2004 Archdiocese of Chicago: Liturgy
Training Publications, 1800 North Hermitage Avenue,
Chicago IL 60622-1101; 1-800-933-1800, fax 1-800-
933-7094, e-mail orders@ltp.org. All rights reserved.
See our website at www.ltp.org.

Audrey Novak Riley was the production editor of this
book. The design is by M. Urgo, and the typesetting was
done by Kari Nicholls in Sabon and Lithos. Cover photo
© 2003 Photos.com.

Printed in Canada.

Library of Congress Control Number 2004109387

ISBN 1-56854-560-6

SIGNA

CONTENTS

INTRODUCTION

Thank you for picking up *Signing the Scriptures: A Starting Point for Interpreting the Sunday Readings for the Deaf, Year A.* If this is your first experience working with glosses, you might want to take a look at the explanation of symbols on the next page and the Glossary of Signs beginning on page 181. The symbols tell you how to execute the glosses, and the glossary lists signs that you might not find in a standard ASL-English dictionary.

The goal of this book is not to tell anyone how scriptures *should* be signed. There are as many correct interpretations as there are interpreters. But sometimes we find ourselves signing in English-language order just because we can't think of a clear way to express the concept in ASL. This book is intended to provide a fresh view and stir up some new ideas for interpreting those sometimes challenging texts. Although the readings are arranged according to the order of the Catholic liturgical year, the index at the back of the book lists all the citations in biblical order, making it easy for anyone to find a specific text.

These glosses have been developed over 20 years. They have been revised, reworked, and tested for clarity and conceptual accuracy, but that doesn't mean they are the *only* way to sign the scriptures. I don't expect anyone to use these glosses exactly as they are written. I hope you will make them your own, adapting them to your own understanding and style, as well as to the language preference of your congregation.

Our mission is to help make God's word accessible to the Deaf and hard of hearing. May God bless you in your ministry.

SYMBOLS

followed by a word in all caps, for example, #ALL • use fingerspelled loan sign

++ • reduplicate the sign two or more times

cl:_ _ • use the given handshapes to show the shape, size, or movement of the named object

? before a sentence • a question mark in the air

?? • crook index finger into a little question mark several times

Exclamation point after a word in the middle of a sentence • sign that word strongly

Numbers in parentheses • list on fingers

Underlined words, for example, <u>Peter</u> • fingerspell the word in the normal way

Words in brackets • may be omitted

Words with a hyphen (-) between, for example, two-of-them • use one sign for the phrase

Words with a tilde (~) between, for example, true~work • two signs flow together

(lh), (rh), (bh) • left hand, right hand, both hands

(l), (r) • place that sign on the left or the right

hon • honorific. Open hand, palm up

^^ • indicates pronoun. Legs

Words in parentheses, for example, (on fingers) • directions to interpreter

FIRST SUNDAY OF ADVENT

BOOK OF THE PROPHET ISAIAH   (2:1–5)

Jerusalem there (r), <u>Isaiah</u> predict what? Future time-period, mountain-tall God establish, his home up-there. #ALL people flock-to-it, tell friends, quote, "Come-on, Lord mountain group-go-up, there God his home, right way he teach us, we follow-him can." There Jerusalem, #ALL people God teach, spread. Country good, bad, he judge; law he give-them will. Their sword change, become farm <u>tools</u>. From-now-on, war—shhh; army training, blow-off-hand. Hey! Live follow Lord.

Word his Lord.

RESPONSORIAL PSALM   (122:1–2, 3–4, 4–5, 6–7, 8–9)

> *We celebrate, Lord his home flock-to.*

I celebrate, why? People inform-me / Lord his home we flock-to
Now we finish touch / Jerusalem gates enter.

Jerusalem, itself city / strong, united
Israel people flock-to-it / group++ different++ group-go.

Law Israel they obey / thank Lord must
There have judgers / who? Family David forever.

Pray for Jerusalem have peace / suppose people love Jerusalem, succeed will they
Peace touch Jerusalem / every building have success.

My family, friends there, / I say, "Peace touch Jerusalem"
Lord God, his house there / I pray good happen there.

LETTER OF PAUL TO THE ROMANS (13:11–14)

Brother~sister, you know-that now time wake-up, why? Near-future God save us. All-night finished, now almost sunrise. Means what? Dark actions, sin, push-aside; light face-to-face. Action appropriate for day—sex, drunk, promiscuity, lust, argue, jealous, shhh. Body desire, throw-out, Jesus Christ accept.

GOSPEL ACCLAMATION

Alleluia

Lord, your love show-us
Please save-us.

HOLY GOSPEL ACCORDING TO MATTHEW (24:37–44)

Jesus story, quote, "Long-ago, time-period <u>Noah</u> (l) . . . future time-period myself come again (r) . . . same-as-it. Long-ago (l), before flood, before, people eat, drink, marry, enjoy. <u>Noah</u> himself boat have, but those people know-nothing. Wrong happen, water flood destroy-them. (body shift) Future time-period (r), happen Son [of] Man come (cl:1) again, same-as-it. Men two work farm, one take-up, left-there one. Women two work, one take-up, left-there one. Means what? Wake-up, pay attention! Lord come when, don't know. Suppose your house, thief plan steal, you finish know time he show-up, you eyes-wide-open (cl:c,c), ready defend. Same must you eyes-wide-open, ready meet Lord, time you predict not."

Gospel his Lord.

IMMACULATE CONCEPTION

BOOK OF GENESIS
(3:9–15, 20)

Tree, fruit, <u>Adam</u> eat; finish, Lord God call-out, "Where you?" (Adam) "You here <u>garden</u>, I hear, but afraid—why? I naked, hide." (God) "Oh-I-see. Who inform-you naked you? Maybe fruit you eat from tree that-one I prohibit?" (Adam) "Woman you put-here, fruit she give-me, so I eat." Lord God question-to woman, "Fruit you eat—why?" (Woman) "Snake, he butter-up-hit. I eat." Snake, Lord God tell-him, "You awful action—punish what? From-now-on, #ALL other animals reject-you; you must stomach crawl-like-snake (cl:1), soil eat. Self, woman, enemy. Your children, her children, enemy. Her son <u>foot</u> you bite (left bite right); he (right stomp on left)." <u>Adam</u> name wife <u>Eve</u>—why? She mother for every person from-now-on.

RESPONSORIAL PSALM
(98:1, 2–3, 3–4)

New song sign-ASL-to Lord; he finish wonderful action.

New song sign-ASL-to Lord / he finish wonderful action
His right hand win succeed / himself mighty.

#ALL people Lord himself save / #ALL countries his judge~fair he show-around
He up-to-now kind, faithful / people Israel he cherish.

People all-over earth / finish see God save us
#ALL country sing happy for Lord / sign-ASL, praise.

LETTER OF PAUL TO THE EPHESIANS
(1:3–6, 11–12)

Praise God, himself father <u>of</u> our Lord Jesus Christ. God give-us every spirit blessing from heaven—how? Give-us Christ. Before God made world, before, he choose us become holy, sin none. Past, he plan adopt us become his children—he think-self—for-for? Want #ALL people praise him because he love us, give us Christ. So, God choose us with Christ, connect; God cause everything happen++ follow his plan, his want; his glory he want us praise—how? Believe, trust Christ.

GOSPEL ACCLAMATION

Alleluia

Hello, Mary, yourself inspire grace, Lord touch-you
Bless you than other women.

HOLY GOSPEL ACCORDING TO LUKE (1:26–38)

Angel name <u>Gabriel</u>, God send touch town name <u>Nazareth</u>, visit virgin, herself near-future marry man name <u>Joseph</u>, himself family <u>David</u> descend. Virgin, her name <u>Mary</u>. Angel come-down (cl:1), said, "Celebrate! God with you, bless you special want!" She confused, not understand. (Angel) "Fear, wave-no. God satisfy you. You will pregnant, born son, name-him Jesus. People honor-him, call-him Son of God Most High. Lord God give-him authority same David, his ancestor. He control people Israel forever; his control completed never."

Mary question, "How possible? I marry not-yet, me." (Angel) "Holy Spirit touch you will, power his God Most High inspire you. Your holy baby true~work son his God. Know-that <u>Elizabeth</u>, your cousin, herself old, now pregnant. People think she pregnant can't (^), but now sixth month pregnant. God expert action anything!" (Mary) "Serve Lord I willing. Go-ahead, happen same you recent story." Finish, angel leave~dissolve.

SECOND SUNDAY OF ADVENT

BOOK OF THE PROPHET ISAIAH

(11:1–10)

Long-ago family <u>Jesse</u>, generation-forward++, future born child. Lord, his spirit touch-him (child), inspire wise, oh-I-see, understand, power. Spirit teach-him know, respect Lord. Happen Lord he honor, happy he. He child grow-up, judge how? Appearance look-at? No. Gossip hear++? No. People poor, he judge fair, decide best for them. People bad, he bawl-out, order kill-them. He continue faithful, fair always. Finish, wolf, sheep socialize will. Tiger, goat peace. Calf, lion, eat~graze together. He child lead them. Cow, bear, live near, their children play socialize. Lion, cow, same hay eat. Baby play snake, it bite-him none. Here my holy mountain, people hurt each-other none, why? #ALL know Lord. Future day, he child show-up. Non-Jews search-for him will, why? His home full glory.

Word his Lord.

RESPONSORIAL PSALM

(72:1–2, 7–8, 12–13, 17)

Future time-period, your king judge fair, peace forever.

God, there king, please give-him wise / king son, give-him judge fair
Your people, he control fair / those poor, he mercy-them.

Your king judge fair-around will / give peace forever
All-over world king himself control / from here river all-over earth.

Poor man cry-out, king save-him / have help none, king help
Poor, humble, trivial, he mercy-them / their life, he save.

His name, honor forever / his name continue until sun dissolve
#ALL people he bless / #ALL people happy, praise him.

Everything up-till-now jot-down, for-for? Teach us, hope give us, how? Bible teach-you patience, encourage-you. God himself expert patient, encourage. I pray he help-you live harmony~united-around, follow Jesus Christ. Succeed, your heart united-around, voice united-around, glory give-to God, himself Father (of) Lord Jesus Christ. Christ accept you, same you accept each-other must, for-for? Glory give-to God. Inform-you, Christ became servant theirs Jews for show-you God his long-ago promise now satisfied true. Non-Jews, they praise God because he mercy-them. Bible show, quote, "Non-Jew people I socialize, praise you; your name I honor."

Word his Lord.

GOSPEL ACCLAMATION

Alleluia

Prepare way for Lord, straight
#ALL people see God save us.

HOLY GOSPEL ACCORDING TO MATTHEW (3:1–12)

Area Judea, John Baptizer show-up, preach what? Quote, "Your life change! God kingdom near-future." Long-ago, Isaiah write about him (John), quote, "Informer announce, prepare way for Lord, make straight-way for him." John dress camel hair (itchy), belt-around-waist. He eat what? bugs (grasshoppers) and honey. People all-over-area flock-to see-him. Sin they confess, he baptize-(immerse)-them river Jordan. Jew higher-ups several come forward (cl:1,1), want immerse. John tell-them: You snake, you! God punish, you try escape? You intend life change? Proof where? You brag, "My father, Abraham." So-what? Stones themselves, God can change-them become children his Abraham. Right-now, ax ready chop-down-tree, why? Suppose tree fruit #NG, chop-down, throw-on-fire. I immerse-in water for show honest life change; but later other person show-up, himself powerful! than me. His shoes I touch, not worthy enough, me. He immerse you Holy Spirit and fire will he. He now ready good, bad separate. Good, save; bad, throw-in fire.

Gospel his Lord.

THIRD SUNDAY OF ADVENT

BOOK OF THE PROPHET ISAIAH

(35:1–6, 10)

Land dry, empty, it celebrate will. Field bloom++ flowers different++, sing. Land become beautiful same there area name Lebanon, there area name Carmel [there area name Sharon]. Lord his glory, his beauty people see will. Hands-hang-down, knees-shake, no! Become strong. People their heart afraid, tell them, quote, "Become strong, afraid none! Your God there. He comes ready defeat++ (others), save you." Finish, people blind see can, people deaf hear, people crippled run same deer, people can't talk, they sing will. God save his people. Home [to] Zion they come, sing, happy forever. Sad, grief, good-riddance.

Word his Lord.

RESPONSORIAL PSALM

(146:6–7, 8–9, 9–10)

Lord, please save-us.

Bless God, he faithful forever / (2) people oppressed, he judge fair
(3) People hungry, he feed / (4) slave, he give-them free.

People blind, Lord give-them see / people humble, he raise-up
People live right, Lord love them / know~new~person, he protect.

Father none, widow, Lord care-for-them / but, person bad, he punish
Lord, he control forever / your God forever and ever. Alleluia!

LETTER OF JAMES

(5:7–10)

My brother~sister, continue patient. Lord come will. Notice farmer, he patient wait grow++. Winter, spring rain, he patient wait, rain, cherish grow. Same must you patient. Give-up, no-wave, Lord near-future come. You complain each-other, finish—why? God look, maybe judge you, you, you guilty #ALL. He judger ready come. You suffer, difficult; patient accept how? Remember prophets long-ago they preach Lord, whew suffer awful. Continue patient—follow their.

Word his Lord.

GOSPEL ACCLAMATION

Alleluia

God his spirit touch-me, he finish choose-me
People poor, inform-them happy.

HOLY GOSPEL ACCORDING TO MATTHEW (11:2–11)

John Baptizer stuck jail, hear gossip Jesus wonderful #do-do; disciple he send question-him, quote, "John predict important man show-up. That-one you, or wait other someone must we?" Jesus tell-him, "Go, inform John you finish see: (1) blind, see can; (2) crippled, walk again; (3) sick, healed; (4) deaf, hear; (5) dead, live again; (6) people poor, inform-them good news. Person himself accept me, bless-him." Away-they-go; Jesus story about John. "You flock-to desert, for-for? See something grow (cl:1) wave, wind blow-over? Tell-me honest, you want see what? Man dressed ritzy? Remember, people dressed ritzy tend live king house. So, you flock-to desert, why? See prophet want? Yes, right. John himself prophet plus more. Long-ago Bible story, quote, "I send him informer first; prepare way for God son will he." Inform-you, John himself most important man up-to-now, but there heaven, last trivial person beat-him (shot-h)."

Gospel his Lord.

FOURTH SUNDAY OF ADVENT

BOOK OF THE PROPHET ISAIAH

(7:10–14)

King name <u>Ahaz</u>, Lord tell-him, quote, "Ask Lord God give-you proof. Ask me show-you something from heaven (or) from hell, either-one." (Ahaz) "Refuse me. Test God, refuse me!" Isaiah tell-him, "You people, you stubborn, bore me; same Lord, bore-him. Lord himself give-you proof—what? Virgin hit pregnant will, born son, name-him <u>Emmanuel</u>."

Word his Lord.

RESPONSORIAL PSALM

(24:1–2, 3–4, 5–6)

Accept Lord, himself king glory

Lord he control whole earth / #ALL people, animals, control
Ocean there, world he make, put (in ocean) / splash! River flow-out.

Lord his mountain who climb, / Lord his holy place who stand, who?
Person himself sin none, heart clean / earth things cherish not.

Lord his blessing give-him (downward to good person) / God success give-him
Same happen #ALL people seek God / cherish God (of) Jacob.

LETTER OF PAUL TO THE ROMANS

(1:1–7)

Hello from <u>Paul</u>, myself servant his Christ Jesus. God summon-me, choose-me, for-for? become apostle, gospel that-one long-ago he promise through prophets, I preach must. Bible itself story God son, human family <u>David</u> descended, but true Son [of] God. He full power because spirit holy touch-him, cause-him die, resurrect live again. Who he? Jesus Christ our Lord. He summon-us become apostles, his name preach++, non-Jews recruit++, gather-up-include

Jesus Christ. #ALL-you there Rome, God love you, summon-you become holy. Please God Father and Lord Jesus Christ their grace, peace give-you.

Word his Lord.

GOSPEL ACCLAMATION

Alleluia

Virgin become pregnant will, born son,
Name-him <u>Emmanuel</u>.

HOLY GOSPEL ACCORDING TO MATTHEW   (1:18–24)

Story Jesus born, what? Mother Mary and <u>Joseph</u>, two-of-them engaged but live together not-yet, Mary hit pregnant—how? Holy Spirit cause. Joseph himself good man; take-her court, punish, don't-want. #Do-do? Private divorce decide. He bed sleep, wrong happen visualize angel tell-him, "Go-ahead, marry Mary. She pregnant, how? Holy Spirit cause. Born son will she, name-him Jesus must you— why? People he save, no-matter they sin." Recent story happen, for-for? Long-ago, Lord promise virgin hit pregnant, born son, name <u>Emmanuel</u> [means God with us]. Joseph wake-up, angel command obey, accept Mary married.

Gospel his Lord.

CHRISTMAS VIGIL

BOOK OF THE PROPHET ISAIAH

(62:1–5)

<u>Zion</u> I love, silent refuse me. Jerusalem I love, I talk continue until its good shines compare sunrise, until its success shows compare candle. Your success, #ALL nations will see; your glory, #ALL kings will see. Lord himself give-you name new. You compare beautiful crown for God. Past, people name-you, quote, "Abandoned"; your land they name, quote, "Empty." But now people name-you, quote, "God cherish"; your land they name, quote, "God wife." Lord love you, your land want marry. Pretty girl, young man marry; same God marry you. Wife, husband cherish; same God cherish you.

Word his Lord.

RESPONSORIAL PSALM

(89:4–5, 16–17, 27, 29)

Forever I sing, Lord himself good

God say, "My special person I finish promise / Himself <u>David</u> my servant.
Your family I support generations / your kingdom continue forever."

Those people, good news they know, happy they / they walk face-to-face (God)
Your name they hear, happy / you judge-fair, bless-them.

David will say, "Yourself my Father / My God, my support, my savior."
God kindness continue forever / God promise stand-strong.

ACTS OF THE APOSTLES

(13:16–17, 22–25)

Synagogue (s-y like church) Paul enter, said, "Israel people, #ALL honor God, pay-attention-me. Long ago, our ancestors, God choose.

During time there Egypt, he help them; later, he lead them out safe. God choose David become king, why? He said, "David have heart same-as-mine, follow my want will he." Now generations-forward, born Jesus, himself savior for Israel. John prepare Israel people for Jesus arrive, how? Baptize, change life. John preach, say, "Myself Messiah not. Other man come will. Touch his shoes, I not worthy enough."

Word his Lord.

GOSPEL ACCLAMATION

Alleluia

Tomorrow, here earth sin, God destroy,
Savior for world take-up control will.

HOLY GOSPEL ACCORDING TO MATTHEW

(1:1–25)
(Shorter: omit text in brackets)

[Jesus, his pass-down-generations, begin Abraham up-till-now:
Abraham born Isaac, pass-to Jacob,
pass-to Judah and brother,
pass-to Perez and Zerah, their mother Tamar,
pass-to Hezron, pass-to Ram,
pass-to Amminadab, pass-to Nahshon
pass-to Salmon, pass-to Boaz, his mother Rahab,
pass-to Obed, his mother Ruth
pass-to Jesse, pass-to King David.

David born Solomon, his mother ex-wife Uriah,
pass-to Rehoboam, pass-to Abijah,
pass-to Asaph, pass-to Jehoshaphat,
pass-to Joram, pass-to Uzziah,
pass-to Jotham, pass-to Ahaz
pass-to Hezekiah, pass-to Manasseh
pass-to Amos, pass-to Josiah,

13

pass-to Jechoniah and brother during time-period slave there Babylon.

Slave time-period finish, Jechoniah born Shealtiel,
pass-to Zerubbabel, pass-to Abiud,
pass-to Eliakim, pass-to Azor,
pass-to Zadok, pass-to Achim
pass-to Eliud, pass-to Eleazar
pass-to Matthan, pass-to Jacob, his son Joseph, that-one Mary marry. She, Mary, born Jesus Christ.

Altogether generations how-many? Abraham to David, fourteen. David to time-period slave, fourteen. Time-period slave to Jesus born, fourteen.]

Now story Jesus born: His mother Mary engage man name Joseph, understand, married not-yet, herself hit pregnant, how? Holy Spirit cause. Joseph good man, punish her don't-want; private divorce decide. Wrong, dream, angel show-up, tell-him, "Fear none, go-ahead marry; Mary pregnant how? Holy Spirit. She will born son. Name-him Jesus must you, why? His people he save."

Recent story happen for-for? Long-ago prophet write: "Virgin will hit pregnant, born son, name-him Emmanuel." [Word means, "God with us."]

Joseph wake-up, obey angel, two-of-them marry. Two-of-them sex never until born son, name Jesus.

Gospel his Lord.

CHRISTMAS, MIDNIGHT MASS

BOOK OF THE PROPHET ISAIAH (9:1–3, 5–6)

People past live dark, now see bright-light; past live land obscure, now light-shine-down. God give-them happy, celebrate. They celebrate face-to-face-God same harvest time, excited money share-around. Why? Their burden, their suffering, God destroy same past, (day of Midian). Time-period war, finished. Clothes bloody, burn~dissolve.

Now, baby born; son God give-us. He take control will. They name-him, quote, "(1) Wonderful Counselor, (2) God-Hero, (3) Father Forever, (4) Prince (of) Peace." His kingdom huge, have peace forever. David his kingdom, he (son) support continue, judge-fair now and forever. Lord enthusiastic action these-things (on fingers).

Word his Lord.

RESPONSORIAL PSALM (96:1–2, 2–3, 11–12, 13)

Today born our Savior, Christ Lord.

New song sign-ASL-to Lord / Sing for Lord, #ALL people
Sing for Lord / his name honor.

Every-day, announce he save us / his glory inform #ALL people
All-over world / his wonderful work announce.

(1) Heaven happy, earth celebrate / (2) Ocean, fish sing, happy
(3) Field, animals celebrate / (4) #ALL trees excited, happy.

They (on fingers) happy why? Lord finish come / He come for control take-up
World, he control fair-around / People, he control faithful.

LETTER OF PAUL TO TITUS

(2:11–14)

God his grace now here, for save #ALL people. Grace teach-us what? Sin, world thirst, push-aside; live right, holy during wait, hope see glory his God and Jesus, our Savior. Jesus himself sacrifice die for us, save us, our sin forgive; now we his people true, enthusiastic action right.

Word his Lord.

GOSPEL ACCLAMATION

Alleluia

I inform-you wonderful happen:
Today born Savior, Christ Lord.

HOLY GOSPEL ACCORDING TO LUKE

(2:1–14)

Long-ago, controller name <u>Caesar Augustus</u> order #ALL people all-over count. So each person go-to town where his family generations-back start. <u>Joseph</u> live there <u>Nazareth</u>, go-to town name Bethlehem— reason? Himself family <u>David</u> descend—wife Mary, two-of-them go, understand, Mary herself pregnant. During there, happen time give-birth baby. Mary give-birth, cloth wrap-up, manger lay-him-in— Why? There house travelers stay all-night, full, room have none.

Near area, shepherds work watch all-night. Angel from Lord show-up, glory shine-down (2h); they afraid! Angel tell-them, "Afraid, nothing. I inform-you wonderful happen, good #NEWS for #ALL people. Today, recent there Bethlehem, born Savior, himself Messiah, Lord. Proof what? Manger, you go-to-it, notice baby, cloth wrap-up, lay-in." Wrong, angels many! hordes sing praise God, quote, "Glory give-to God heaven, peace touch earth for people he cherish."

Gospel his Lord.

CHRISTMAS, MASS DURING THE DAY

BOOK OF THE PROPHET ISAIAH (52:7–10)

Person walk mountain, his feet cherish—who he? That-one person good inform bring, peace announce, inform happy, announce save, and tell #ALL people, "Your God true King!" Hey! Your prophet shout, together shout happy—why? They see, visualize: Zion, Lord again establish. Jerusalem, itself finish destroyed, now again sing happy—why? Lord his people he comfort; Jerusalem he save. Lord his holy power show, #ALL people see. God save his people, #ALL countries see will.

Word his Lord.

RESPONSORIAL PSALM (98:1, 2–3, 3–4, 5–6)

All-over earth, people see God expert save.

New song sign-ASL-to Lord / he finish wonderful action
His right hand win succeed / himself mighty.

#ALL people Lord himself save / #ALL countries his judge~fair he show-around
He up-to-now kind, faithful / people Israel he cherish.

People all-over earth / finish see God save us
#ALL country sing happy for Lord / sign-ASL, praise.

Sing praise Lord with harp (cl) / song, voice, praise
Trumpet loud, music / happy sign-ASL-to Lord, King.

LETTER TO THE HEBREWS (1:1–6)

Long-ago, our ancestors God speak-to obscure—how? Prophet preach. Now, God speak-to us through his Son. God, with Jesus, two-of-them universe make, set-up, share equal. Father his glory,

Jesus show; two-of-them exact same, wrong none. Our sin, Son remove; finish, heaven go, sit, control with God. Angels, he beat (shot-h); their name, his name beat. ? God tell angel, "You my son; today I become your Father"?? No, never. Happen God his first-born Son send go-to world, he say, "#ALL angels worship him must."

Word his Lord.

GOSPEL ACCLAMATION

Alleluia

Now morning holy day
Come, #ALL people, worship Lord
Today earth, light shine-down.

HOLY GOSPEL ACCORDING TO JOHN (1:1–18)

Before world begin, before, Jesus himself with God, Jesus himself true~work God. Everything, he make++. Jesus give life; life cause light. Dark, no-matter, light shine, beat-it (shot-h). Man name <u>John</u>, God send, for-for? Inform people about Jesus. Himself Jesus not, but his duty teach about Jesus, that-one come, light give for world. World Jesus touch—world himself make—but world don't-know who he. People accept-him not. But people few accept-him; those, he give-them power become children his God. Suppose people believe his name, mother-father not~need. They born from God himself.

Jesus become human, live here earth. His glory we finish see, God his Son, full grace and honest. <u>John</u> preach about him, said, "Remember I tell-you other person come, himself important than me? That-one he." Jesus give-you grace increase++. Moses give law, but Jesus give grace, honest. See God, impossible; but Jesus himself show-you God.

Gospel his Lord.

HOLY FAMILY

BOOK OF SIRACH

Father, Lord put-him-there, children honor must; mother, God give-her authority control son. Suppose person honor father, his sin God forgive; respect mother, wonderful things God reserve for him. Honor father, many children will you; happen you pray, God pay-attention. Person honor father, live from-now-on long; person comfort mother, that-one obey Lord. My son, happen your father old, care-for him; cause-him grief not. Suppose father mind-weak, patient. Yourself strong, make-fun-of-him not. Why? You kind-to father, God remember. Later you sin, God forgive.

Word his Lord.

RESPONSORIAL PSALM

(128:1–2, 3, 4–5)

#IF Lord you honor, his wants follow, bless you.

#IF Lord you honor, his want follow / he bless you
Your work succeed, you benefit / God bless you, cherish you

Your wife many children born +++ / there your home
Your children grow++ / table they sit-around (cl: crooked v, v)

Suppose Lord you honor / God bless you same
There heaven, Lord see, bless
Hope see Jerusalem succeed / during your life, forever.

LETTER OF PAUL TO THE COLOSSIANS (3:12–21) (Shorter: omit text in brackets)

God choose you special, holy, cherish. Now must you become mercy, (2) kind, (3) humble, (4) sweet, (5) patient. Accept each-other, complain++ push-aside; forgive, same Lord finish forgive you. Last, must you love—why? Love cause these (on fingers) become perfect.

19

Christ his peace control your heart. You united one body, peace must you. Always thank-him (God). Christ, his word true important; allow his word inspire you. Happen your wisdom become perfect, teach each-other. Sing thanks-to God from your heart, psalm and holy songs sign-ASL-to-God. Any #do-do, no-matter talk, action—honor name Lord Jesus. Thank God Father through Jesus. [You wives, humble obey husband—why? Your duty. Husband, love wife, anger, hate none. Children, you-all obey parents every way—reason? Lord satisfy. Fathers, you-all bawl-out children, no-wave. They maybe feel discouraged.]

Word his Lord.

GOSPEL ACCLAMATION

Alleluia

Christ his peace your heart control,
His word touch-heart, grow, succeed.

HOLY GOSPEL ACCORDING TO MATTHEW   (2:13–15, 19–23)

Kings three leave finish, Joseph sleep, dream, envision angel tell him, quote, "Wake-up. Three-of-you escape there Egypt must. Why? Jesus, Herod search-for, want kill-him." Joseph get-up, family take, three-of-them group-go Egypt, stay until Herod die. Long-ago prophet write, quote, "My son I summon from Egypt"—true happen. Herod die, angel tell Joseph, "Now three-of-you #BACK Israel safe, why? King dead." Joseph obey, family go-to Israel. But Joseph hear gossip Herod son become king, he afraid. He dream, decide go-to area name Galilee, there town name Nazareth. Long-ago prophet write, quote, "He shall live town name Nazareth." True happen.

Gospel his Lord.

Blessed Virgin Mary, Mother of God

BOOK OF NUMBERS (6:22–27)

Moses Lord inform-him, quote, "Tell Aaron and his son bless Israel people how? Say: 'Lord bless you, protect you. Lord his face shine-down-on-you, mercy-you. Lord kind look-down kind, peace give-you.' Pray finish, bless-them will I."

Word his Lord.

RESPONSORIAL PSALM (67:2–3, 5, 6, 8)

God please mercy-me, bless-me.

God please mercy-me, bless-me / his face shine-down-on-me
Finish, his action here we know / he save us, #ALL people know.

#ALL people / celebrate happy—why?
Because God control-them fair / #ALL people he lead right.

#ALL people praise-you God / #ALL countries praise you
God please bless us, / #ALL people see, honor-him (God)!

LETTER OF PAUL TO THE GALATIANS (4:4–7)

Happen time right, God send son, born from woman; understand, son himself follow law must. His duty what? Law remove. Finish, true become children his God can we. You true children God— proof what? Spirit same his son, God put-in-heart, spirit cry-out Abba (means Father). You slave, no, push-aside; now son. Everything give-you, God want.

Word his Lord.

GOSPEL ACCLAMATION

Alleluia

Long-ago, God speak-to people how? Prophets.
Now God speak how? His son speak.

HOLY GOSPEL ACCORDING TO LUKE   (2:16–21)

There Bethlehem shepherds hurry, find Mary and <u>Joseph</u>; there manger, baby. Succeed (pah!) understand recent inform-me about it baby. Shepherds out, inform++; #ALL listen, mouth-drop-open.

Mary see happen++, memorize, wonder-about. Shepherds go #BACK, glory give-to God, for-for? Everything they recent see, hear.

Eighth day, time circumcise, baby name-him Jesus—why? Long-ago, conceive~pregnant not-yet, angel tell Mary baby name Jesus.

Gospel his Lord.

EPIPHANY OF THE LORD

BOOK OF THE PROPHET ISAIAH

(60:1–6)

Jerusalem, rise-up, shine! Glory from Lord shine-down-on you. See, earth dark, people obscure; but you, Lord shine-down, glory. Other countries people walk can because your bright-light; your radiance, kings they see. Look, they flock-to-you, your sons and daughters. You will see, inspire! Your heart flutter, overflow. Ocean, wonderful things pour-out-to-you. Other countries, their wealth bring-to-you. Camels line-up flock-to-you [from Midian and Ephah]; from Sheba they bring gold and sweet-whiff, announce praise Lord.

Word his Lord.

RESPONSORIAL PSALM

(72:1–2, 7–8, 10–11, 12–13)

Lord, #ALL people here earth worship you.

King, please give-him wise judge / king son, give-him judge~fair
Your people, he control fair / your people poor, he mercy-them.

#ALL people he judge fair will / give peace forever
All-over earth king himself control / from here river to far area.

Kings theirs countries different++ / they bring-him gift, gold
#ALL kings honor-him / #ALL people serve him.

Person poor cry-out, he save-him / person weak, alone, he help
Humble, poor, he mercy-them / their life he save.

LETTER OF PAUL TO THE EPHESIANS

(3:2–3, 5–6)

You know-that God finish give-me ministry for you. Secret plan God have, people long-ago know-nothing; but now apostles and prophets, Holy Spirit inform-them. His God plan what? Through Christ Jesus, non-Jews, Jews, now same, member same body connect, same promise share through gospel preach.

Word his Lord.

GOSPEL ACCLAMATION

Alleluia

Star we see rise (sunrise)
We come for honor king.

HOLY GOSPEL ACCORDING TO MATTHEW (2:1–12)

Jesus born there Bethlehem during King <u>Herod</u> reign. Now Jerusalem, star watchers from east arrive, question, "Where baby new king theirs Jews, where? Star rise we noticed, come here, honor want." King <u>Herod</u> disgruntled, Jerusalem people same. Religious leaders king summon, question where Messiah born. (Leaders) "Bethlehem [there <u>Judea</u>]. Long-ago prophet write, "Bethlehem true important town [in <u>Judah</u>]—why? it will born controller, himself lead my people Israel."

Star watchers <u>Herod</u> summon, question-them time star show-up, exact time what? Finish, tell-them, "Go, baby find. Learn whatever, come inform-me. Go honor-him, I want."

Three-of-them depart. Star follow (cl:1,3) until stop up-there, down-there house, baby there. Three-of them happy, enter, baby with mother Mary see, kneel, honor. Bring-box, take-off-lid, give-him gold, next-to-that sweet-whiff, next-to-that oil perfume.

Later, three-of-them sleep, dream, visualize, "<u>Herod</u> inform not." Close-vision, decide go home different way.

Gospel his Lord.

Baptism of the Lord

BOOK OF THE PROPHET ISAIAH

(42:1–4, 6–7)

Here my servant; I support-him, satisfy me. My spirit, I give-him. #ALL countries he judge fair will; quiet he, shout not. New grow, he walk, crush not. Cute candle, he "snuff" not. Establish judge~fair here earth will he; his teach #ALL people wait-for.

Myself Lord; I summon-you for help judge~fair succeed; I lead you, teach you, I establish you for relationship-with-God, you compare light for #ALL people. Blind, see will; prison, free; stuck dark, out.

Word his Lord.

RESPONSORIAL PSALM

(29:1–2, 3–4, 3, 9–10)

#ALL people, Lord bless, give-them peace

#ALL people connect Lord, everything give-him / praise, glory give-to-him Respect, glory give-to-him / #ALL worship Lord.

Lord his voice spread-out / his voice touch water-area
His voice noisy / Lord his voice mighty.

God his glory thunder / there (heaven) people announce glory
Lord, himself, king there heaven / Himself king forever.

ACTS OF THE APOSTLES

(10:34–38)

Cornelius with people hordes his house, Peter preach-to-them: quote, "Now I understand, oh-I-see, #ALL people God love equal, none prefer special. Any person from any country, he respect God and action right, God accept-him. That-one God inform people Israel, good #NEWS, peace, same Jesus Christ announce, himself Lord over #ALL. I think you finish know rumor, what? There Galilee Jesus baptize; later, Holy Spirit power God give-him. Jesus traveled-around, work good, cause heal, sin forgive; understand, God accompany."

Word his Lord.

GOSPEL ACCLAMATION

Alleluia

Heaven open, Father voice loud:
He my cherish son, pay-attention him.

HOLY GOSPEL ACCORDING TO MATTHEW (3:13–17)

<u>Galilee</u>, Jesus arrive, see <u>John</u> Baptist there. Jesus want him (John) baptize (use "immerse" variation) him (Jesus). <u>John</u> "No! Must you baptize me." But Jesus tell-him, "Please. You baptize me, God want." (John) Gulp, patient~accept, baptize. Head (cl:s) under-water, come-up, (whoa!) heaven open, Spirit flutter-down compare bird, touch Jesus. Hear voice say, "He my son cherish. Satisfy me."

Gospel his Lord.

ASH WEDNESDAY

BOOK OF THE PROPHET JOEL   (2:12–18)

Lord says: "Come #BACK-to me; your heart give-me, with fasting, cry, grieve. Sin push-aside, come-to Lord your God." Himself full mercy, kindness, slow become angry, punish don't-want. Maybe he will mercy-us, bless us. Sacrifice give-to Lord your God. Blow-horn there <u>Zion</u>! Announce fasting; summon meeting; #ALL people assemble, (1) old people (2) children (3) babies assemble. Man, woman wedding near-future, suspend; priest cry, say, "Lord, save your people. Please punish us not; other countries oppress-us, they say "Your God where?"

Finish, Lord heart-soft; people, he mercy-them.

Word his Lord.

RESPONSORIAL PSALM   (51:3–4, 5–6, 12–13, 14, 17)

Lord, we finish sin, please mercy-us

Mercy-me, God, yourself good / yourself heart-soft, my sin forgive
My guilt wash-clean / my sin please remove.

My sin I confess / my wrong I mind-dwell-on
Against you I finish sin / bad things I action, you see-me.

Heart clean give-me, God / spirit strong put-in-me
Reject-me not / your Holy Spirit take-from-me not.

Give me happy, save me / a spirit willing give-me
Lord, give-me sing / sign-ASL praise you will I.

SECOND LETTER OF PAUL TO THE CORINTHIANS (5:20—6:2)

We speak in-exchange Christ, means God speak through us. I beg you, yourself connect God. Jesus himself sin none, but God cause-him become full sin—for-for? Connect Jesus, we can become holy same-as God. God give-you grace, ignore not. God said, "Happen right time, I pay-attention you. Right day, I save you." Right time, now! Right day, now!

Word his Lord.

GOSPEL ACCLAMATION

Praise Lord Jesus Christ, king glory forever.

Heart clean give-me, Lord
Give-me happy, save me.

HOLY GOSPEL ACCORDING TO MATTHEW (6:1–6, 16–18)

Disciples, Jesus tell-them, "You religion actions—warning. Suppose other people see you, God praise-you not. Example, suppose money donate, don't announce, 'Hey, look at me! I donate' same hypocrite. They (people) praise, finish. Better secret donate, none know; God see, praise-you. Suppose you pray, don't stand pray voice loud, people look-up-and-down (cl:f), yourself proud same hypocrite. Better pray secret, door closed, pray Father. God praise-you will. Suppose you fasting, don't expression frown, sad, hungry same hypocrite, people pity-them. Better you fasting, comb-hair, smile, people don't-know you fasting, but God knows. He praise-you will."

Gospel his Lord.

FIRST SUNDAY OF LENT

BOOK OF GENESIS

(2:7–9; 3:1–7)

Dirt~soil Lord God scoop-up, man make (mime), blow-on-him, he become alive. Finish, trees, flowers Lord God put there <u>Eden</u>, man put-there. Trees various grow++, beautiful, good food. Middle, there have tree for life and tree for know good, bad. Animals many; snake itself smart. There woman, snake question-to her, "True~work, God tell-you #ALL trees eat fruit prohibit?" (Woman) "Oh, #ALL fruit eat can; understand, tree middle, God say suppose eat, die." (Serpent) "Die not. God know-that suppose you eat, you become <u>god</u> same-as-him, you know what good, what bad." Tree middle, woman look-at, see fruit delicious, plus become wise want. She take-fruit (cl), bite; husband there, she-give-him, he bite. Quick, two-of-them notice themselves naked, embarrassed. Leaves sew, put-on-clothes.

Word his Lord.

RESPONSORIAL PSALM

(51:3–6, 12–14, 17)

Lord, we finish sin, please mercy-us.

God, mercy-me, yourself good / yourself heart-soft, my sin forgive.
My guilt, please take away, / my sin, please forgive.

My sin, I confess, / my wrong mind-dwell-on always
Against you I finish sin / my actions awful, you see

God, heart clean please give-me / spirit strong put-in-me
Please reject-me not / your holy spirit take-from-me not

Give-me happy, save me / a spirit willing give-me
Lord, give-me sing / sign-ASL praise you will I.

LETTER OF PAUL TO THE ROMANS

Brother~sister, one man (l) cause sin, it sin cause die, means #ALL people die must. Before law, before, law establish not-yet, no-matter, world have sin. We think, none law means none sin—wrong. Adam to Moses, #ALL people die, why? Adam sin influence. #BUT God (r) give different. Adam, his sin give #ALL die, but God fine-wiggle give more! He give Jesus Christ for save #ALL. Adam sin cause judge, punish, but God give forgive. Adam sin cause death succeed, but suppose you accept grace, Jesus Christ forgive you, live forever. One sin means #ALL people hell should, but one good action give forgive for #ALL. Adam disobey, cause #ALL become sinner; Jesus obey, cause #ALL become holy.

Word his Lord.

GOSPEL ACCLAMATION

Praise Lord Jesus Christ, King glory forever.

Bread alone give-you life not;
God his word give-you life.

HOLY GOSPEL ACCORDING TO MATTHEW

Holy Spirit lead Jesus there desert, for-for? Devil tempt. Forty days, nights Jesus fasting, hungry! Devil show-up, question-to-him, "Suppose you true~work God his son, command rock change bread." Jesus tell-him, "Bible says, Bread alone not enough for live. Word his God require." Devil bring Jesus there Jerusalem, temple roof stand (cl:^^), say, "Suppose you true Son of God, go-ahead jump-off, why not? Bible say, "God send angel care-for you; their hands support-you, allow you hurt never." (Jesus) "Bible says, "Test Lord your God, prohibit." Now devil lead Jesus mountain high, #ALL kingdoms world spread-out show-him, tell-him, "All-that

I give-you—understand, you bow-down, worship me (hon)." Jesus say, "Away! Bible says, "Worship God only must you, none other." Devil gulp, leave. Wrong, angels flock-down, care-for Jesus.

Gospel his Lord.

Second Sunday of Lent

BOOK OF GENESIS

(12:1–4a)

Abraham, Lord tell-him, "Your home depart, go-to place I show-you. I cause-you become large nation will I. I bless-you, your name become famous, many people you bless will. Any person bless-you, I bless-him. Any person curse you, I curse him. #ALL countries you bless will." Abraham accept, obey, go.

Word his Lord.

RESPONSORIAL PSALM

(33:4–5, 18–19, 20–22)

Lord, mercy-us, only-you we trust.

Lord, he teach right / his work, we trust can
Judge~fair-around, good actions, he cherish / all-over earth, his kindness spread.

Those people honor Lord, he see / he kind-to-them, they hope
Die? He save them / Hungry? He feed them, they trust.

We patient wait-for Lord / himself help-us, protect-us
Lord, please mercy us / you only we depend-on.

SECOND LETTER OF PAUL TO TIMOTHY

(1:8b–10)

Cherish friends, suppose you suffer for gospel, accept. God give-you strong. He finish save us, summon-us live holy, why? Because we expert good actions? No. Long-ago, he himself plan save-us. Succeed, Jesus Christ show-up, death destroy, life forever give.

Word his Lord.

GOSPEL ACCLAMATION

Praise Lord Jesus Christ, King glory forever.

Cloud, shining, Father his voice speaks,
He (hon) my son cherish, pay-attention him.

HOLY GOSPEL ACCORDING TO MATTHEW (17:1–9)

Jesus with <u>Peter</u>, <u>James</u>, <u>John</u>, four-of-them group-go mountain.
Jesus himself change. Face sparkle, clothes white, wow. <u>Elijah</u>,
Moses, show-up, three-of-them chat. <u>Peter</u> tell Jesus, "Lord,
three-of-us mouth-drop-open. We build tent three for you++."
Wrong, cloud over. They hear voice say, "He (hon) my cherish son;
satisfy me. Pay-attention him." Three-of-them (apostles) kneel~bow-
down, afraid. Jesus tap-on-shoulder, said, "Rise-up, afraid not."
They look-up, see Jesus alone. Four-of-them group-go-down, Jesus
tell-them recent happen announce not until Jesus die, resurrect finish.

Gospel his Lord.

THIRD SUNDAY OF LENT

BOOK OF EXODUS

(17:3–7)

People thirst water, disgruntled, tell Moses, "Egypt you force-me leave, for-for? Here water none, we die, our children, animals die." Moses pray-to-God, "#Do-do, me? Those people ready kill-me." Lord answer, "Go there with Israel leaders few, staff (cl:s,s) yours carry, there rock I stand. You staff-hit-rock, water flow-out, people drink can." Moses go, hit-rock, Israel people watch. That place name <u>Massah</u> and <u>Meribah</u>, why? There Israel people argue, wonder, "God here with us, <u>or</u> not, which?"

Word his Lord.

RESPONSORIAL PSALM

(95:1–2, 6–7, 8–9)

Suppose today God inspire you feel, resist not.

Come, happy sing sign-ASL-to Lord / praise him our savior
Give-him thanks face-to-face / happy sing for him.

Come, bow-down, worship / kneel face-to-face Lord / himself made us
Himself our God / he cherish care-for us.

Suppose today God inspire you feel / resist not same long-ago
There desert your ancestors doubt / God work they see, no-matter, skeptical.

LETTER OF PAUL TO THE ROMANS

(5:1–2, 5–8)

Now faith have, means we peace connect-to God with Jesus Christ. Faith Jesus give-us, now grace we receive can, and we boast, why? Glory his God we hope see. We hope . . . disappointed not. God his love inspire us, his Holy Spirit he-give-us. Past, time right, happen we weak sinners, Christ died for us. Suppose person true~work good, maybe friend brave willing die in-exchange, possible; but God prove love, how? We sinners, no-matter Christ died in-exchange.

Word his Lord.

GOSPEL ACCLAMATION

Praise Lord Jesus Christ, king glory forever

Lord, #ALL people you save true,
Live~water give me, I thirst again never.

HOLY GOSPEL ACCORDING TO JOHN   (4:5–42) (Shorter: omit text in brackets)

Town name <u>Samaria</u>, there near <u>Jacob</u> <u>well</u> (cl:circular, sides) Jesus arrive. Jesus tired, sit-down, time noon. Woman come (cl:1) for-for? Water draw-up. Jesus tell-her, "Water cup-give-me." Disciples finish go-out town, food buy. Woman say, "Myself woman <u>Samaritan</u>, you Jew, you ask-me for drink, why?" Understand, Jew, <u>Samaritan</u>, two-of-them get-along not. Jesus tell-her, "Suppose you know who I (hon), you will ask me for drink, and live water I give-you." (Woman) "You bucket none. Well deep. Water you draw-up how? This well, our ancestor <u>Jacob</u>, his family, drink, he give-us. You important beat-him (shot-h)?" (Jesus) "This water drink, thirst again will. My water drink, thirst again never. Water I give for live forever." (Woman) "Wow, your water give-me. Every-day come++ for water draw-up, bore me."

[(Jesus) "Go, husband bring-here." (Woman) "Husband none me." (Jesus) "Right—husband none you. You married five times, but man live with now, married not. You speak honest."]

(Woman) "Hey, yourself prophet. Hm. Our ancestor worship God here mountain, but Jew say worship there Jerusalem must." (Jesus) "Near-future, people worship God mountain, Jerusalem, no-matter. You worship, but you understand nothing. We understand—why? God save people through Jew generations. But near-future, true believer worship Father through Spirit and honest—those believers Father want worship him, why? Father himself spirit, means people worship-him want, themselves full Spirit and honest must."

Woman said, "I know-that Messiah will come, that-one name Christ, he will tell us everything." (Jesus) "That-one me (hon)."

[At-that-moment, apostles arrive, shock, why? Woman, Jesus chat-with. They question-to-him "Why? What-do?"—shhhh. Woman herself depart, town go-to, people tell, "Come, see man, he tell-me everything I action up-to-now—possible he Christ??" People curious, flock-to-him.

Jesus, apostles urge-him eat. Jesus tell-them, "I have food, you know-nothing." They puzzled, who bring-him food? Jesus inform-them, "My food what? Follow God his want, his work complete. You say, quote "Four months future, time harvest." Well, I inform-you, ready harvest now. Those people live forever, harvest them; finish, planter and harvester celebrate together. True, one person plant, other person harvest. You plant nothing, I send you for harvest. People previous work, preach finish—now you recruit succeed."]

Many people start believe Jesus because woman story, quote, "He tell-me everything I action up-to-now." Now people meet-him, invite-him stay. Jesus stay two-days. More people start believe, tell woman, "Past, your story we believe, but now myself finish see Jesus, know-that himself true~work savior for world."

Gospel his Lord.

FOURTH SUNDAY OF LENT

FIRST BOOK OF SAMUEL

(16:1, 6–7, 10–13)

<u>Samuel</u>, Lord tell-him, quote, "Oil pour-in-bottle, go-to <u>Jesse</u> there Bethlehem—why? His son I choose become king." <u>Samuel</u> see his (Jesse's) son name <u>Eliab</u>, think, "Wow, Lord choose-him." But Lord say, "You see-him tall, muscular, think thumbs-up, but I thumbs-down. People look-up-and-down (cl:f,f), think face-good, but God see his heart." Son seven <u>Jesse</u> bring, but <u>Samuel</u> tell-him, "God choose none. Other son have?" (Jesse) "Son young care-for sheep." (Samuel) "Summon-him. Sacrifice, feast suspend, wait he arrive." Son, <u>Jesse</u> summon-him. Himself face-nice, strong. Lord said, "That-one anoint." <u>Samuel</u>, oil anoint-him <u>David</u>; from-now-on God his spirit influence-him, inspire.

Word his Lord.

RESPONSORIAL PSALM

(23:1–3a, 3b–4, 5, 6)

Lord, himself my care-er, give-me everything I need.

Lord, he my care-er, give-me everything I need / there grass area, he give me rest;
Near quiet river, he lead me; / my soul he inspire.

Right way he lead-me for his name honor
Suppose dark valley I walk (cl:1), / no-matter, afraid nothing.
He here with-me, accompany, full power, might / courage give-me.

Banquet he prepare, my enemies look-at-me / my head he anoint; my cup (lh) fill-up-overflow.
God good, kind, touch my life / die, I live there his home for ever and ever.

LETTER OF PAUL TO THE EPHESIANS

Brother~sister, past, you dark, but now Lord give-you light. Live right, why? Light give things good, right, honest. Learn how satisfy Lord. Dark, bad actions, hands-off. Those actions bad, must you shine-on, show, become bright, good. Quote, "You sleep, wake-up. Dead, arise. Christ give-you light."

Word his Lord.

GOSPEL ACCLAMATION

Praise Lord Jesus Christ, king glory forever.

Lord says, "Myself light for world.
Any person follow me, light for live I give-him."

HOLY GOSPEL ACCORDING TO JOHN   (9:1–41) (Shorter: omit text in brackets)

Jesus walk (cl:1), notice man himself blind up-to-now, grow-up.

[Disciples question-to-him, "He blind, why? Himself sin, or his parents sin, which?" (Jesus) "None sin. He blind for God power show. God send me (hon) work for him during day light. Happen night, dark, work impossible. Myself light for world."]

Jesus spit-on-ground, mix, mud (mime smearing on man's eyes), finish, tell-him, "Go there pool name Siloam, wash-face." Man go, wash, #BACK, see can. People near-area habit see-him beg, said, "Man past sit beg, that-one he?" Some said yes, that-one he; other said no, face-same, but true different. Man himself say, "Yes, that-one me!"

[People question-to-him, "Now you see, how?" (Man) "Man name Jesus, mud he mix, my eyes smear-on, tell-me wash, now I see." (People) "Oh-I-see. Where Jesus, where?" (Man) "I don't know."]

Now, people grab-him, put-him face-to-face Pharisee group. [That day, Sabbath, means work prohibit.] Pharisee question-to-man how

38

possible see? Man again explain story. They said, "Jesus come from God not—why? He honor Sabbath not." But some said, "Suppose he sinner, wonderful work how?" Again man, they-question-to-him, "Jesus cause-you see—your opinion what?" (Man) "Prophet he."

[He blind up-to-now, now see can, Jews skeptical! Parents summon, question-to-them, "This your son? Himself true~work born blind? Now he see. How possible?" Two-of-them answer, "He our son, yes, blind up-to-now, yes, but how see, puzzled. Self question-to-him. He old enough, answer-you can he." Understand, parents fear Jews. Suppose two-of-them admit Jesus true Messiah, Jews kick-them-out. So, two-of-them answer, "Self question-to-him."

Again man summon, tell-him, "Glory give-to God. That Jesus, he sinner." Man answer, "He sinner, I don't-know. I know one thing. Past I blind, now I see." (Jews) "He #do-do? Cause-you see, how?" (Man) "Finish I tell you, again not~need. You up-to-now ignore-me— now become follower want?" (Jews) "You follow him, not me. We follow Moses. We know-that God talk-to Moses. God talk-to him? Skeptical!" (Man) (cl: between-the-eyes), "Oh-I-see, you skeptical, but he give-me see. We know-that suppose sinner pray, God ignore, but suppose good, holy person pray, God pay-attention. Other person cause blind become see, where? None! He from God, give-me see!"]

(Jews) "What? Yourself sinner up-to-now, you preach-to-us?" Grab-him, throw-him-out. Story~rumor Jesus hear, search, meet, said, "You believe son of man?" (Man) "I willing believe—where?" (Jesus) "You finish see. That-one me (hon)." (Man) "Yes, I believe." Kneel, worship.

[Jesus said, "I come-down-to (cl:1) world for-for? Judge. Those blind become see; those see become blind." Pharisee hear, question-to-him, "You mean we blind?" Jesus answer: "Suppose you true~work blind, none sin. But you say 'We see can,' means you sin have."]

Gospel his Lord.

FIFTH SUNDAY OF LENT

BOOK OF THE PROPHET EZEKIEL

(37:12–14)

God says, quote, "My people, your grave, I open, raise-you live again, bring-you Israel, why? You know-that myself Lord, happen grave open, you rise, live again. My spirit, I give-you; your land, I put-you-on; finish, you know-that myself true~work Lord. I finish promise; true happen will."

Word his Lord.

RESPONSORIAL PSALM

(130:1–2, 3–4, 5–6, 7–8)

Lord himself mercy-us, save us

Myself suffer, I cry-out (to Lord) / my cry please pay-attention.
Lord, please, pay-attention / my sign-ASL, my prayers.

Suppose you, Lord, remember sin / who innocent, who
But you forgive us / want us honor you.

I trust Lord / his promise I believe
Guard wait for dawn / same Israel wait for Lord.

Lord himself mercy-us / save-us he willing.
Israel he save / their sin forgive.

LETTER OF PAUL TO THE ROMANS

(8:8–11)

Brother~sister, your body actions satisfy Lord can't (^). But you depend body not; you depend spirit, why? God his spirit live in you. Any person himself have none spirit, he connect God not-yet. But, suppose Christ live in you, your body sin, compare dead; but your spirit live still. Happen Jesus die, God raise-him live again. Suppose God spirit live in you, happen you die, God raise-you live again same.

GOSPEL ACCLAMATION

Praise Lord Jesus Christ, King glory forever.

Lord says, "Myself resurrect, live
Any person believe me, suppose he die, no-matter, live will."

HOLY GOSPEL ACCORDING TO JOHN   (11:1–45) (Shorter: omit text in brackets)

[There town name <u>Bethany</u>, woman name <u>Mary</u>—that-one perfume pour, Jesus feet wash, hair dry-feet, that-one—with sister name <u>Martha</u>, their brother name <u>Lazarus</u>, he sick.]

Lazarus, his sisters, two-of-them send inform Jesus their brother sick. Jesus hear, said, "He die not. He sick for-for? Glory give God, my-turn glory me (hon)." Understand, three-of-them Jesus love, but two-days postpone. Finally, he tell apostles, "Now <u>Judea</u> we go-to."

[Apostles argue, "Jew people kill-you want. Better not go." Jesus tell-them, "Day have twelve hours. Suppose person walk during day, fall-down not, why? Light. But suppose person walk during night, fall-down, why? Light have none. Our friend <u>Lazarus</u> now sleep, but I wake-him will." (Apostles) "Suppose he sleep, safe he." Know-that, Jesus mean die, but they think he mean normal sleep. Jesus tell-them straight, "<u>Lazarus</u> finish die. I happy, why? Now you believe will. Come-on." <u>Thomas</u> said, "Fine. Die with you accept."]

Arrive, Jesus find <u>Lazarus</u> bury four-days up-to-now. [That town, Jerusalem near, many people flock-to, pity <u>Mary</u> and <u>Martha</u> because brother die.] Jesus arrive, rumor <u>Martha</u> hear, go-to meet-him. <u>Mary</u> stay home. She (Martha) say, "Lord, suppose you here, my brother die not. Now, suppose you pray, God pay-attention." Jesus tell-her, "Your brother live again will." (Martha) "I know-that last day resurrect will." (Jesus) "I myself give resurrect, live; suppose person believe me, he die, no-matter, live will. You believe me??" (Martha) "Yes, Lord, now I believe yourself Christ, son of God, touch here world."

[Finish, she go-to sister <u>Mary</u>, tell her, "Jesus there want see you."
<u>Mary</u> quick go (cl:1), meet—understand, Jesus touch city not-yet,
stay-there, wait. There house, Jew friends see <u>Mary</u> go-out, they
flock-after, guess~feel she go-to grave. <u>Mary</u> walk (cl:1), Jesus meet,
kneel face-to-face-him, say, "Lord, suppose you come quick, my
brother die not." She cry.]

Jesus look-at-her, heart-touch, himself become upset, said, "Body
bury where?" Jew people say, "Come, see." Jesus cry. People say,
"Wow, friend he cherish"—but some people say, "Blind, he cause-
them see. Friend heal, why not?"

Jesus again upset, arrive grave, itself <u>cave</u> (cl), rock cover-entrance.
Jesus say, "Rock push-aside." <u>Martha</u> tell-him, "Four-days up-to-
now. Stink." (Jesus) "Finish I tell-you, suppose you believe, see God
his glory will you." Stone push-aside. Jesus pray, "Father, I thank-
you pay-attention-me. I know-that you always pay-attention-me, but
now people see, believe you finish send-me here." Finish, Jesus cry-
out loud, "<u>Lazarus</u>, come!" Wrong, man come (cl:1), wrap (like
mummy, arms folded across chest, mime), face covered. Jesus said,
"Unwrap him (mime), go-off."

Now Jews many see, believe.

Gospel his Lord.

Palm Sunday of the Lord's Passion

HOLY GOSPEL ACCORDING TO MATTHEW (21:1–11)

Jesus with disciples group-go Jerusalem, Jesus tell disciples two, "Town ahead, go there, find young donkey two. Lead-to here. Suppose someone ask you #do-do, tell-him, "Two-of-them, Jesus need, but near-future give #BACK." That happen for-for? Long-ago prophet write, 'See, your king arrive humble, donkey ride-on.' Two-of-them go (cl:V), donkey find, lead-to Jesus, coat throw-over-back, Jesus mount. Many people coat throw-on-ground, other people tree branch-break-off, throw-on-ground. People shout, "Hosanna! Son his <u>David</u>. Honor him come name Lord. Hosanna high!" Jerusalem, Jesus arrive, people ask who he? Answer, "He Jesus, prophet from <u>Nazareth</u> [there <u>Galilee</u>]."

Gospel his Lord.

BOOK OF THE PROPHET ISAIAH (50:4–7)

Lord God teach-me, give-me skill lecture; those people tired, I preach, cause-them excited. Every-morning, God help-me pay-attention-him, and I resist not, ignore not. People beat me, I patient accept; they pluck-beard mine, I offer more; they spit-on-me, I shield-face not. Lord God help-me, I embarrassed not. I stand-strong, know-that I ashamed not.

Word his Lord.

RESPONSORIAL PSALM (22:8–9, 17–8, 19–20, 23–24)

My God, you abandon me—why?

#ALL see me, mock-me/ they laugh-out-loud, shake finger side-to-side, say "He (man) trust Lord. If he (God) love him (man), / let's-see him (God) save him (man)."

Many sinners there (point l and r) / they close-in (cl 4:4)
My hands, feet nail, nail, nail, / my bones hurt, hurt, hurt.

My clothes they share-around / for my coat they throw-dice,
let's-see who win
Please, Lord, stay near / hurry help-me.

Your name I proclaim-to #ALL people / audience face-to-face
I praise you
"Suppose you honor Lord, praise him / you people Israel,
give-him glory."

LETTER OF PAUL TO THE PHILIPPIANS (2:6–11)

Attitude same Christ must you. Jesus himself true~work God, but he
cherish it (point upward) not. No, he humble born same slave, same
us. Himself full human. He obey, accept die cross. Now, God raise
him live again, give-him name, #ALL other names exceed. Hear Jesus
name, every person kneel, there heaven, here earth, under earth,
every voice announce, give glory God Father: Jesus Christ true Lord!

Word his Lord.

GOSPEL ACCLAMATION

Praise you Lord Jesus Christ, King glory forever!

Christ himself obey Father, willing die there cross
Now God raise-him-up, honor,
give-him name, #ALL other name exceed.

PASSION OF OUR LORD JESUS CHRIST ACCORDING TO MATTHEW (26:14—27:66)

One apostle, his name <u>Judas Iscariot</u>, he go-to religious leader,
ask, "Suppose Jesus I hand-over-to-you, you pay-me how-much?"
They pay-him silver coins thirty; now he wait, jump-at-chance.

Approach time Passover, disciples few question-to Jesus, "Passover dinner we cook where?"

Jesus tell-them, "Town there, go-to, tell man, "Your house, teacher wants Passover celebrate there."

Disciples go, dinner cook there.

Night, Jesus eat with apostles twelve, say,
"Know-that, one (of) you will betray-me."

#ALL upset, said, "Not me."

Jesus answer:
"Yes, himself now eat with me, he betray-me will. Must happen, why? Long ago write about me. But pity that-one man he betray-me. Better he never born."

Judas look-at-Jesus, say, "Not me, Lord?" Jesus answer,
"You say it."

During eat, Jesus bread take-up, thank-God, give-out, said,
"Take, eat, this my body."
Finish, wine cup take-up, thank-God, give-out, said,
"Drink this, #ALL, this my blood, means new promise~connect.
Blood I lose for many, their sins forgive. I inform-you, wine I drink again not here earth. Future I drink with you there heaven."

They sing; finish, go-to Mountain Olives. Jesus inform-them:
"You since faith me, but tonight doubt will—why? Prophet write, 'Happen shepherd I kill, sheep scatter.' But later, I resurrect, meet-you there Galilee will I."

Peter tell-him,
"Maybe they doubt, but I doubt never."

Jesus tell-him,
"I promise, before rooster crows morning, before, you will three times deny know me."

<u>Peter</u> said,
"I willing die with you. Deny never."
Apostles #ALL said same.

Arrive place name <u>Gethsemane</u>, Jesus tell apostles,
"Sit here; I go over-there, pray."

Jesus, with <u>Peter</u> and other apostles two, four-of them walk (cl:4).
Jesus feel upset, tell-them,
"My soul sad, ready die. Stay here, awake."

He walk-away (cl:1), kneel, pray,
"Father, suffer die, I don't want. But your will I accept."

Finish, Jesus come #BACK, find apostles asleep, said,
"One hour awake can't? Ready, pray none test you. Your spirit
willing, but human body weak."

Again Jesus go (cl:1) pray,
"My father, suppose I suffer must, your will I accept."
Again come #BACK, they asleep. They sleepy—shrug.
Third time Jesus go pray, #BACK, said,
"Still asleep? Now time hand-me-over those sinners. Wake-up,
come-on. My betrayer here."

<u>Judas</u> arrive with people many, they have sword, club (mime). <u>Judas</u>
tell-them,
"Man I kiss, that-one arrest."
He walk-to (cl:1), said, "Hello, Rabbi," kiss.
Jesus said,
"Friend, go-ahead action."

They grab-him (Jesus).
One apostle draw-sword, swing; servant, his ear cut-off. Jesus tell-him,
"Sword, put-in. Suppose you sword-stab, other person sword-stab
you. Suppose I call-out Father, twelve million angels he send for
help-me. But Bible predict, satisfy must I."

Jesus tell people,
"You come sword, club, for-for? Every-day there temple I sit, teach, you arrest-me never. But now Bible you follow, arrest-me must."

Apostles afraid, escape.

Jesus, they lead-him face-to-face Caiaphas, himself priest-most, and other Jew leaders few. Peter follow, priest-most area enter, sit-down, let's-see happen. Jew leaders question-around, try find story prove Jesus die must, but have none. Many people lie about Jesus, but their++ story conflict++. Succeed, two people said,
"He said temple he destroy, three days build again can."

Priest-most question-to Jesus:
"You answer none?"

Jesus silent. Priest-most tell-him,
"I order-you tell-me honest, yourself true~work Christ, Son his God?"

Jesus answer,
"Self say that. But inform-you, future I with God there heaven, see will you."

Priest-most said,
"Witness need none. You hear him lie. Decide what?"

They answer,
"Die must."

They spit-on-him, slap-him, said,
"Guess who hit-you."

Peter still sit outside area. Girl~servant said,
"You here with Jesus."

But he deny,
(Peter) "Wrong you."

Later, other girl notice-him, said
"That man follow Jesus."

Again <u>Peter</u> deny,
(Peter) "I don't-know that man not-yet."

Later, other person say,
"Know Jesus you must, two-of-you talk same."

<u>Peter</u> curse,
(Peter) "I know him nothing!"
Quick, rooster crow; <u>Peter</u> remember Jesus little-story,
"Before rooster crow, you will three times deny know me."
Gulp, cry.

Time morning, Jew leaders decide what #do-do. Hands tie-up, lead face-to-face <u>Pilate</u>, himself governor.

Time-same, <u>Judas</u> see what~happen, sorry. Money give-#BACK, said, "I sin, for-for? Jesus himself innocent."

(Jews) "So what? Self responsible."
Money he throw-down, out, hang-himself. Jew priest said, "Money save can't, why? Dirty."

#Do-do? Decide buy land for foreign people bury. Now that land name, quote, "Field <u>of</u> Blood." That satisfy long-ago <u>Jeremiah</u> prophecy, quote, "Thirty coins worth equal one man, they pay for field, same Lord command."

Now Jesus face-to-face governor, he (governor) question-to him (Jesus), "Yourself king theirs Jews?"

"Self say that."

Jew leaders they blame-him++, but Jesus answer nothing. Pilate question-to-him,
"You see they blame-you?"

But Jesus answer none. They shocked.

Every-year time Passover, Pilate habit allow one prisoner out free—who? People think-self. One prisoner awful, his name <u>Barabbas</u>. Pilate question-to people,

"Barabbas you want out free, or king yours Jews, which?"

Understand, he know Jew leaders jealous, want Jesus die. He sit, wait; wrong, wife send inform-him, "That good man, hurt not. I finish dream about him, afraid me." Jew leaders urge people better ask-for Barabbas out free, Jesus kill. Pilate question-them, "Out free, which?"

They answer, "Barabbas!"

(Pilate) "Jesus Christ, #do-do me?"

(People) "Crucify him."

(Pilate) "Why? Wrong what?

They more shout, "Crucify him."

Pilate want people calm-down. He bring water~bowl, hands wash, say, "Hands-off, me. Yourselves decide."

(People) "His blood we accept responsible."

Barabbas out free, Jesus send-away for beat, finish, hand-him-over for crucify. Soldiers lead Jesus large room [name Praetorium], Jew leaders hordes. Clothes remove, red clothes they put-on-him, crown sharp thorns make, put-on-head, long-stick give-him, mock-him, say, "Honor King Jews!"

They spit, hit-him, mock. Finish, red clothes take-off, his clothes put-on, lead him for crucify. One man name Simon, they force-him help cross carry.

Arrive Golgotha [name means Place of Skull], wine they give-him. Jesus taste, drink refuse. Crucify finish, his clothes share++ how? Roll-dice. Finish, they sit, watch. Poster Jesus wrong what? Quote "King theirs Jews." Two other men crucified right (cl:1), left (cl:1).

People walk, look-up Jesus, said, "Temple you destroy, build again three days. Save yourself, why-not? Cross come-down!"

Jew leaders said,
"Other people he finish save, but save himself can't. If he true
Messiah, king Israel—come-down now; we see, believe. He trust
God, now let's-see God save him. He name himself God Son."
Two men left, right (cl:1, 1) same make-fun-of-him.

Time noon, happen dark, continue all-afternoon until 3:00. Jesus
cry-out,
"My God, my God, you abandon me, why?"
People few hear, say, "He summon Elijah."

One person go, long-stick (cl:f,f), sponge (cl: something soft) stick-
on-end, wine sour dip-in, hold-up-to-Jesus. Other people said,
"Wait, let's-see Elijah come help-him."
Jesus cry-out, die.

(Kneel in silence)

Quick, temple curtain tear-top-to-bottom. Earth quake, rocks
collapse, grave open, bodies dead resurrect, walk-to city, many
people see-them. These-things (on fingers), soldier see, afraid!
Said,
"This man true~work son his God."

Women several over-there watch, themselves up-to-now follow Jesus,
his needs care-for—who they? Mary Magdalene and friends few.
Time sunset, man name Joseph [from Arimathea] arrive, himself
rich, he brave face-to-face Pilate, ask-for body Jesus. Pilate "OK."
Body take-down, cloth wrap-around, rock-grave lay. Finish, rock
(big) roll cover-entrance. Women sit, watch. Tomorrow day, Jew
leaders tell Pilate, "Remember Jesus said three days finish, resurrect?
Better you order three-days grave watch, why? Maybe his followers
body steal, hide, tell people he true~work resurrect. Lie!"

Pilate agree, so they go, seal-it (cl:A around seam of entrance),
plus watch.

Gospel his Lord.

HOLY THURSDAY

BOOK OF EXODUS

(12:1–8, 11–14)

There Egypt, Moses, Aaron, Lord tell-them, quote, "Now month must move-to-thumb, become first month (of) year. People Israel, inform-them what? From-now-on, this month tenth day must every family lamb take-up. Suppose it family small, share with other family can. Lamb itself must boy, age-one, perfect, wrong none. Can either sheep, goat, either. Reserve, four days wait; finish, time sunset #ALL people gather, lamb there++, kill++. Blood take home (cl:container); door post, lintel, blood rub-on. Same night, meat cook, eat with bread flat and bitter herbs. Eat how? Full clothes, shoes, staff (cl) hold, idea-same ready escape. Tonight happen Passover of Lord—why? Myself Lord, touch Egypt will I, every firstborn person and animal, I kill. Egypt people I judge, punish. But your house blood have (smeared-on). I see, pass. Egypt people I destroy, but touch you nothing. This day must you future remember, look-back, celebrate every-year forever."

Word his Lord.

RESPONSORIAL PSALM

(116:12–13, 15–16bc, 17–18)

Our wine bless, itself become true blood his Christ.

Many good things Lord action for me / I pay-him how?
Cup holy wine, I drink will / Lord his name I summon.

Faithful follower die / Lord see, heart-touch
Myself your servant, same-as my mother / but you give-me free.

I sacrifice, thank-you / Lord his name I summon.
Lord I finish promise, succeed / #ALL people see can.

FIRST LETTER OF PAUL TO THE CORINTHIANS (11:23–26)

Lord inform-me, I inform-you—what? Night before Jesus die, before, Jesus bread take-up, pray thank-God, break, said, "This true my body for you. You action this, remember, look-back me." Eat finish, Jesus wine take-up-cup, said, "This cup means new connect through my blood. Every time you drink, remember me." So, every time bread eat, wine drink, you announce Jesus die, until he comes again!

Word his Lord.

GOSPEL ACCLAMATION

Praise Lord Jesus Christ, king glory forever.

Lord says, "New order I give-you:
I up-to-now love you, same you love each-other must.

HOLY GOSPEL ACCORDING TO JOHN (13:1–15)

Time celebrate Passover, Jesus know near-future die, go-to Father. Jesus up-to-now always love his friends and continue love until last. Past, apostle name Judas, devil finish urge-him betray Jesus. Now, during eat, Jesus stand-up, coat-take-off. Understand, Jesus know himself come from God and near-future go #BACK God. Towel, Jesus tie-around-self, bowl, water pour-in; apostle feet wash, dry-with-towel. Take-turns to Simon Peter. He said, "Lord, my feet you want wash??" (Jesus) "Now you understand none; later, understand clear." (Peter) "You wash my feet, nothing!" (Jesus) "Suppose I wash you not, two-of-us disconnect." (Peter) "Lord, please my feet and hands and head wash." Jesus tell-him, "Man finish bath, wash again not~need—only feet wash need. Himself finish clean, same you; but not #ALL." Jesus say not #ALL finish clean, why? He know who will betray-him. Wash finish, Jesus coat-put-on, sit-down, said, "?? You understand what I recent action for you? You name-me Teacher, Lord—right. I true~work Teacher, Lord. But your feet I wash. Mean what? You wash feet each-other must. I show-you example. Same-as-me serve must you."

Gospel his Lord.

GOOD FRIDAY

BOOK OF THE PROPHET ISAIAH (52:13—53:12)

See, my servant succeed will, raise-him-up, honor-him. Many people see-him, shock; his face ruin, not look like true person. Many countries puzzle will, king mouth-drop-open. People they up-to-now never hear about God, they see, wonder. Who can believe what we finish hear? Who can understand Lord his plan? He (servant) grow-up face-to-face God compare young tree grow from ground dry. He look~like strong king not; we fascinate not. People hate, avoid him—true suffer he experience, pain used-to. People ignore-him, reject-him, honor not. But our weakness he accept, our pain he tolerate. We think God punish him . . . wrong. He willing accept punish for our sin in-exchange us. Beating he accept, now we healed; his pain heal us. Past, we compare sheep, think-self, wander (cl:1,1). We guilty, but our sin, God take-off-me, put-on-him. They beat-him awful, but he patient accept, complain none. He quiet, compare sheep~small lead, kill; or sheep~large stand (^^-legs), wait-for shear. They judge him, lead-away, kill, and who think more about him? Finish he die for sin theirs people, they bury him area with sinners—understand, himself wrong nothing, lie none. But God himself decide destroy him.

Suppose die for sin he willing, descendents many will he, and God his plan succeed will. Because he suffer, he future touch heaven. Through suffer, my servant cause many people connect God; their sin, their punishment he accept. So I honor-him, why? He patient accept die. People think himself sinner, but true sin theirs he remove, and God forgive them.

Word his Lord.

RESPONSORIAL PSALM

(31:2, 6, 12–13, 15–16, 17, 25)

Father, my spirit I-give-to your control.

Lord, you I trust / allow me shame never
Yourself judge fair, save me / my spirit I-give-to your control.
Lord, yourself save me, / my faithful God.

My enemies mock-me / people laugh-at-me, friends un-popular
They see me walk (cl:1), escape / they forget me, feel myself compare
same dead, worthless.

But I continue trust Lord / yourself my God
My life you control / my enemy persecute-me, you save me.

Please look-at-me, shine-on-me / yourself kind, save me
Hey, yourselves brave, stand-strong / #ALL you trust Lord.

LETTER TO THE HEBREWS

(4:14–16; 5:7–9)

Our priest-most finish touch heaven—who? Jesus, son his God.
Please continue faith. Our priest-most understand our weakness
can, why? He experience tempt same-as-us, but sin never. Now
we confident go (cl:1) face-to-face God, pray, know-that he mercy,
love, help-me time I need help.

Past time-period during Jesus live here earth, he cry, pray God help-
him, save life, die not. God pay-attention him—why? He (Jesus)
honor him (God). Jesus himself God son, but learn how obey through
suffer. Now he perfect; #ALL people they obey him, save them can he.

Word his Lord.

GOSPEL ACCLAMATION

Praise Lord Jesus Christ, king glory forever.

Christ himself obey, willing die there cross.
Now, God raise-him-up, honor,
give-him name, #ALL other name exceed.

PASSION OF OUR LORD JESUS CHRIST
ACCORDING TO JOHN

(18:1—19:42)

Jesus, with disciples, group-to to <u>Kidron</u> <u>Valley</u>, garden there. That place <u>Judas</u> know, why? Jesus and disciples meet there often. <u>Judas</u> arrive with soldier and Jew leader few. They have lantern (cl), torch, sword. Jesus finish know what will happen, step forward (cl:1), said,

You search-for who?

(Jews) "Jesus from <u>Nazareth</u>."

Myself (hon).

Remember, <u>Judas</u>, he there. Happen Jesus say "Myself," #ALL step-back, fall-down. Again Jesus question-them,

Want who?

(Jews) "Jesus from Nazareth" (sign N-town).

I finish tell-you, that me (hon). Let them go-out.

That happen for Jesus promise satisfy: People you (God) give-me I lose one not-yet.

<u>Simon</u> <u>Peter</u> draw-sword; slave there, swing sword, ear #OFF. Slave, his name <u>Malchus</u>. Jesus tell <u>Peter</u>,

Put-in-sword. Obey Father plan, must I.

Soldiers and leaders arrest Jesus, hands tie, bring-him face-to-face
<u>Annas</u>, himself father-in-law him <u>Caiaphas</u>, priest-most. That-one
<u>Caiaphas</u>, past, he encourage Jews pick one man die for #ALL Jew
people. Jesus (cl:1), <u>Simon</u> <u>Peter</u> with other disciple, two-of-them
follow (cl:1, V). He, other disciple, priest-most know him, allow him
enter, <u>Peter</u> left outside gate. Other disciple go-to woman there gate,
chat, succeed open, "Come on!" <u>Peter</u> enter. Woman question-him,

(Woman) You follower his?

(Peter) Not me.

Night cold, servants, soldiers make fire, gather-around, warm rub-
hands. <u>Peter</u> go-there (cl:1), warm rub-hands. Time-same, priest-most
question Jesus about disciples, then about his teach. Jesus answer,

I since preach open. I always teach there temple area, #ALL Jews
gather, nothing secret. Question-me, why? Those people hear me
preach, question-them. They know what I say.

Wrong, soldier slap-him (cl:1), slap face, said,

"Priest-most, you rude-to-him, for-for?"

(Jesus) Suppose I speak wrong, proof where? Suppose I speak
honest, why slap-my-face, why?

Finish, <u>Annas</u> send Jesus face-to-face priest-most name <u>Caiaphas</u>.

Time-same, <u>Peter</u> still warm rub-hands. People question-him,

(Woman) "You Jesus disciple?"

(Peter) "Not me."

One slave, himself cousin that-one ear cut-off, said,
"I finish see you with Jesus there garden."

Again <u>Peter</u>, "No!" Quick, rooster crow. Gulp.

Time sunrise, Jesus they-lead-him there court. Jew people themselves enter, shhh—why? Not pure. Suppose enter, <u>Passover</u> eat can't. <u>Pilate</u> (sign: P-government) come-out (cl:1), say,

"Accuse-him what?"

(Jews) "Law he break, we hand-to-you."

(Pilate) "Self judge him, follow your law, why-not?"

(Jews) "We kill person, prohibit."

Remember Jesus predict how will die? That-one.

Court Pilate again enter, question-him Jesus, "?? Yourself king theirs Jews?"

(Jesus) "You, self interested, or other people inform-you about me, which?"

(Pilate) "Jew nothing me! Your people, your priest-most hand-you-to-me. Wrong #do-do you?"

(Jesus) "My kingdom here world not. Suppose my kingdom here, my people will fight save me, allow hand-me-to Jews, refuse. But my kingdom not here."

(Pilate) "Oh-I-see. Mean you true-work king?"

(Jesus) "You name-me king. I born here world what-for? Teach truth. Any person himself truth cherish, my teach he pay-attention."

(Pilate) "Truth! What mean truth?"

Finish, Pilate again come-out (cl:1), announce Jew hordes, "My opinion, that man innocent. Remember your tradition: every-year, time Passover, one prisoner I allow out free. ?? You want king theirs Jews out free?"

(Jews) "We want <u>Barabbas</u> out free, not Jesus."

Who <u>Barabbas</u>? Rebel.

Now, Pilate send Jesus for beat. Soldiers make sharp++ twist-around, crown-on-head, thorns-dig-in. Purple coat, put-on-him. One-by-one (cl: 1,1) approach-him, slap++, say,
"#ALL honor king theirs Jews!"

Again Pilate come-out (cl:1), tell people,
"Pay-attention-me! Jesus bring here, you look-at-him, see he innocent will you."

Jesus come-out (cl:1) crown-thorns, coat purple.
(Pilate) "There (hon)."

Quick, people see-him, shout,
(Jews) "Crucify him!"

(Pilate) "Selves crucify him. None reason have I."

(Jews) "We have law require he die, why? He name himself God Son."

Pilate hear, afraid. Again court enter, question-him Jesus,
"From where, you?"

Jesus answer none.

(Pilate) "You speak refuse? You know-that I have power, can allow out free, crucify you, think myself?"

(Jesus) "You have power because God give-you power. You sin, but person he betray-me, his sin worse."

Now Pilate enthusiastic Jesus out free, but Jews more shout,
"Suppose you allow Jesus out free, means <u>Caesar</u> you support not. Any person name himself king, he enemy his <u>Caesar</u>."

Their little-story, Pilate hear, oh-I-see. Jesus bring. Sit judge chair, that place name <u>Stone</u> <u>Pavement</u> [Jew word, <u>Gabbatha</u>]. Understand, that day Jew people must prepare for Passover. Now time noon.

Pilate tell-them,
"Your king, there (hon)."

(Jews) "Away! Crucify him!"
(Pilate) "What! Crucify your king?"
(Jews) "Our king Caesar."

Pilate gulp, hand-him-over. They lead Jesus, himself cross carry-on-shoulder; arrive place name Place of (the) Skull [Jew word, Golgotha], crucify him with other men two, right, left (cl:1,1), Jesus middle. Pilate write poster put-over-head (cl) "Jesus from Nazareth, King theirs Jews," language three (1) Jew, (2) Latin, (3) Greek. Many people read poster. Understand, that place, city, near. Jew priest tell-him Pilate,
(Jew) "Hey, better jot-down 'That man name himself King theirs Jews.'"

(Pilate) "I finish write, period."

Jesus crucify finish, his clothes, soldiers share++. Left one coat—#do-do? Tear, don't-want. Decide roll-dice, let's-see who win. Reason? Satisfy Bible verse, "My clothes, they share-around, for my coat they roll dice."

Near cross, there group, who? Jesus his mother, her sister, other friend, and Mary Magdalene. Jesus see mother with disciple best-friend, tell-her,

"Woman, there your son."
Next-to-her disciple,
"There your mother."

From-then-on, he disciple care-for Mary.

Jesus know-that his duty completed, said,
"I thirst."

There jar full cheap wine. Soldier (mime long, skinny reed, soft-thing put-on-end, dip in jar, hold up to Jesus). Jesus taste, said, "Now complete, finish."

Head-bow (cl:s) die.

That day Passover meal Jews prepare must, body (point one, two, three) leave-there cross, don't-want, why? Special holy day. They ask Pilate please their <u>legs</u> break, hurry die, body take-down, carry away. So, soldiers go, man there (r), there (l), swing-club right, left; but Jesus himself finish die, swing-club not~need. One soldier draw-sword, stab-him; wrong, blood, water, flow-down. One witness see happen, he inform for help-you believe. Bible predict finish satisfy, "His bone, break none." Other verse, "They will look-at the person they finish stab."

Later, man name <u>Joseph</u> [from <u>Arimathea</u>], himself secret follower, he ask Pilate, "Don't-mind body I take-down?" (Pilate) Go ahead. (Joseph) Thank you. Take-down-body. Other secret follower, name <u>Nicodemus</u>, he bring oil and <u>spice</u>, container (cl) 100 pounds. Jesus body, wrap++, oil wrap++, follow Jew habit bury. Cross there, almost-nothing there <u>garden</u>, it have new <u>tomb</u>, body put-in-tomb not-yet. Time++, hurry, Jesus body put-in-tomb, leave-there, why? Must dash home, prepare for Passover.

Gospel his Lord.

EASTER VIGIL

FIRST READING: BOOK OF GENESIS

(1:1—2:2)

Begin, heaven, earth, God make++; dark, wind, water messed-up. God said, "Give light!" God see, like, decide light, dark separate, name-it day, name-it night. First day, finish. Now God say, "Water separate (top, bottom) must." Make dome (cl), water above, name sky. Second day, finish. God said, "Water push-together, dry land area." Land name earth, water name ocean. God see, satisfied. Decide grow flower, tree, fruit, various. Pah! Grow++. God like. Third day, finish. Now God say, "Sky need lights during day, night, for-for? Count day, month, year." So, God make sun bright-light for day, and moon, stars small light for night. God look-around, satisfied. Fourth day, finish. God think, say, "Animals, where? Fish, bird, earth need." God make animals various, there ocean swim, there sky fly. God bless-them, tell-them go-ahead all-over earth spread. Fifth day, finish. Now God say, "Earth need animals more, cow, insect, various." Pah, animal <u>wild</u>, cow, insect, snake, various. God happy. Last, God say, "Now man we make, same-as us. Fish, animal, bird, man control will." So, man, woman, God make. He bless-them, tell-them go-ahead, earth spread-out, take-up control. Plus, God give-them tree, fruit, #VEG various for eat; #ALL animals grass, plant eat. Sixth day, finish. Heaven earth, God work six days, make++, finish, seventh day, God #do-do? Rest.

Word his Lord.

RESPONSORIAL PSALM

(104:1–2, 5–6, 10, 12, 13–14, 14, 35)

Lord, your spirit send-down, all-over earth become new.

My soul bless Lord / God himself wonderful true
Yourself full power, glory / clothes shine-out-bright

Earth, yourself make, establish / stand-strong forever
Oceans you group-left, group-right / mountains you set-up.

Rivers you send flow / mountains, flow-around
There, birds live / their song speak-outward-to heaven.

There heaven, you give rain / earth food grow, grow
Grass for animals eat, grow ++ for people / bread make, eat.

Your many actions true wonderful / you wise, make++
All-over earth, you make++ / my soul bless Lord.

or   (33:4–5, 6–7, 12–13, 20–22)

All-over earth show Lord himself good.

Lord his word appropriate / his actions honest
Judge~fair, good action, he love / his kindness touch all-over earth.

Lord himself finish heaven make / angels, he invent, cause
Here earth, water he group-left / ocean group-right.

That country honor Lord, God bless them / he choose them, cherish
Heaven, Lord look-down / #ALL people he see.

We patient wait-for Lord / himself help-us, protect us
Lord, please mercy-us / we depend-on you alone.

SECOND READING: BOOK OF GENESIS   (22:1–2, 9, 10–13, 15–18)

Abraham God test. God call-out, "Abraham!" (Abraham) "What?"
(God) "Your son <u>Isaac</u>, that-one you cherish, two-of-you go place
name <u>Moriah</u>. Arrive finish, I show-you where you kill, sacrifice."
Tomorrow morning, donkey put-on-saddle, son, two-of-them with
servants two, wood carry, start travel. Third day, Abraham see there
place, tell servants stay here, two-of-us go, worship, #BACK. Wood,
son back, put on; walk (cl:1,1) "Father?" (Abraham)"What?" (Son)
"Animal for sacrifice, where?" Gulp. (Abraham) "God give will."

Two-of-them travel, arrive, altar build, wood put-on-altar. Finish, Abraham son put-on-altar, draw-knife, ready stab. But angel call-out "Abraham!" (Abraham) "What?" (Angel) "Kill son not. Hurt not. I know-that you love God, why? Son you willing sacrifice." Abraham look-around, notice sheep there, catch-it, replace-son, kill, sacrifice. That place, Abraham name-it <u>Yahweh-yireh</u>, means, "Lord will see." Again angel call-out, say, "Lord inform-you, quote, "You willing your son kill for me, now I bless you excessively, you have descendants many! same star, same <u>sand</u>. Enemy, your descendants beat (shot-h), give bless for #ALL people—why? Because my order you obey."

RESPONSORIAL PSALM

(16:5, 8, 9–10, 11)

Lord, I trust only-you.

Lord, I cherish-you / my future, you lead, protect
Lord I follow always / God accompany, I afraid nothing.

My heart happy, my soul celebrate / my body "laid-back," confident
I know-that my soul God abandon never / my body he care-for, ruin never.

Way (to) heaven, you show-me / happy with you, will I
Enjoy socialize together / forever, ever.

THIRD READING: BOOK OF EXODUS

(14:15—15:1)

Moses, Lord tell-him, "You complain, for-for? Israel people, tell-them go straight-ahead. Your <u>staff</u> (cl) hold-out, ocean separate will, dry area, people flock-through. Egypt soldiers arrogant, follow, but my glory see will they. Know myself true~work Lord will they.

God, his angel up-to-now lead, now behind, protect. Plus, cloud past front, now behind, obscure. Dark, Egypt people, Israel people look-at-each-other, see none. Moses hold-staff-out, wrong, east wind blow all-night, morning see water separated, dry area (middle).

Israel people flock-through, safe, water left, right. Egypt soldiers follow, horse, wagon flock-through. But Lord give-them afraid, they hurry, stuck <u>mud</u>, wrong, decide back-up, Israel defeat-them don't-want.

But Moses, God tell-him, "Again hold-staff-out, water close will." Moses hold-staff-out, water flow-together, Egypt soldiers stuck, escape can't, #ALL die. Israel people recent walk there dry, water left, right. God save. Israel look, Egypt soldiers dead see, whew! Lord power! They afraid, Lord and Moses they believe. They sing, praise Lord, quote: "I sing for Lord, he wonderful succeed; horse, soldier he throw-into ocean, drown."

RESPONSORIAL PSALM   (Exodus 15:1–2, 3–4, 5–6, 17–18)

We sing sign-ASL-to Lord; himself full glory.

I sing for Lord, himself glory win / horse, "wheelchair~reins,"
he toss-out ocean
Lord himself give-me strong, brave / he finish save me
Himself my God, praise him / my God up-to-now, I worship him.

Lord himself compare soldier / his name quote, LORD!
Egypt king, his "wheelchair~reins" God toss-out ocean /
his expert soldiers, water drown.

Soldiers, water rise, cover-head / they same rock, drown-fast
Lord, you power action it (point to drowned soldiers) / enemy,
you destroy.

But your people, you save / there mountain, you establish home
That place, you decide stay, control / that holy place yourself choose
Lord control forever, ever.

FOURTH READING: BOOK OF THE PROPHET ISAIAH (54:5–14)

Your quote "husband," who? Lord himself, he finish make you. Himself save you. He summon-you, compare young wife, her husband abandon-her, now summon-her #BACK. God says, "Short time, I abandon-you, but now heart-soft, I accept you, love you. Short time, I angry, ignore-you, but now cherish you. Remember time-period Noah, I promise earth flood destroy again never? Now I promise angry again never. Suppose mountain collapse, no-matter, I love you continue." Lord himself mercy-you, peace give-you. Pity my people, they troubled, worried, no-wave; your city I build new, foundation sapphires, walls precious (cherish) rock-shiny. Your tower (cl) I make ruby red sparkle, your gates and walls, diamonds. Your son, Lord himself teach-them; your children peace will. You, I establish, fear none, oppression none, destroy none.

Word his Lord.

RESPONSORIAL PSALM (Psalm 30:2, 4, 5–6, 11–12)

Lord, I praise you, why? You finish save me.

Lord, I praise you, why? You finish save me /
my enemy beat-me (shot-h), you prohibit
Die, you save me / people go-to hell, you grab-me-out.

You faithful people, sing praise Lord / thank-you his holy name
He angry short / but he mercy forever
Time night, cry / but sunrise, celebrate~happy.

Lord, please pay-attention-me, mercy-me / Lord, please help-me
Past, I heart-wring, now you give-me dance / I thank-you forever.

FIFTH READING: BOOK OF THE PROPHET ISAIAH (55:1–11)

Thirsty you-all? Come-here, water. Money none? Come-here, food have. Come, pay none, cost none. Wine, milk drink. Money spend for things can't eat, why? Satisfy not. Pay-attention-me, eat good, enjoy. Come-here me (hon), pay-attention-me, live will you. I again promise connect-to-you, same long-ago I promise united <u>David</u>. Remember <u>David</u>, my power he prove, how? Country different++, he defeat. Same will you. Country you don't-know, you summon; they don't-know you, no matter, come quick, obey. Why? Lord give-you power, glory.

Search-for Lord now, why? Possible find him. Call-to-him now, why? He near. Sinner, life~change must. Sin thought, push-aside. Look-at Lord, ask mercy-me; God forgive always. Lord says, "My thought, your thought, same not. My way, your way, different. Know-that heaven high, earth f-a-a-a-r separate? That compare my way, your way separate; my thought, your thought separate." Know-that heaven water sprinkle-down soil, wet, cause grow++, finish, water rise-up, dissolve. Grow++ make <u>seed</u> for farmer, plus grind-up, make bread for people eat. Same compare my word speak~outward, action++ what I want; finish, #BACK succeed.

Word his Lord.

RESPONSORIAL PSALM

(Isaiah 12:2–3, 4, 5–6)

Happy, celebrate will you, why? God finish save you.

God finish save me / now I afraid nothing.
Lord give-me brave, strong / himself true~work my savior.
Happy, celebrate will you / God finish save you.

Thank-you Lord / his name praise
#ALL people inform-them his actions / his holy name announce.

Sing praise Lord his wonderful succeed / all-over earth inform.
Jerusalem people, shout happy! / Holy God finish touch Israel.

SIXTH READING: BOOK OF THE PROPHET BARUCH (3:9–15, 32—4:4)

Israel people, pay attention. Commandments give-you live. ?? How happen, here foreign country you live, enemy you socialize? God his wise, you ignore, why? Suppose you up-to-now obey God, peace will you. You become smart, strong, understand++, same have long live, light, peace, will you. Who finish succeed wise? Who finish study, understand?

Only God himself true~work wise. God know everything. Earth, he set-up; animal he make++; sunset, sunrise, he order; stars he put++; he summon-them, they happy answer, "We here!" Who compare equal our God, who? None. Everything he understand, <u>Jacob</u> and Israel people he teach.

Now here earth have wise. Wise find where? There book God his Law. Suppose law follow, live; but law ignore, die will. Come, law accept, itself give-you light for live. Honor other <u>god</u> not, follow other religion not. We lucky, why? Satisfy God want, we know how.

Word his Lord.

RESPONSORIAL PSALM

(Psalm 19:8, 9, 10, 11)

Lord, your little-story give-me life forever.

Lord his law perfect / our soul inspire
Lord his decide, trust can / people humble become wise.

Lord his commandment right / cause heart happy
Lord his order clear / we understand can.

Honor Lord true / continue forever and ever;
Lord his law true / #ALL (down fingers) fair.

God law (l), gold heap (r) / worth, which? It (l, law).
Honey sweet, delicious / same his law sweet.

SEVENTH READING: BOOK OF THE PROPHET EZEKIEL (36:16–17a, 18–28)

Lord inform-me, quote, "Israel people, their action awful sin. Angry me, why? They kill++, plus idol worship. I force-them scatter country different++. They arrive, embarrass me; those people know-that my people, I force-them scatter. My holy name, those people make-fun-of; now, mind-change me, heart-soft, my people come #BACK I allow. Tell Israel people, quote 'You come #BACK I allow why? Because I cherish you? No. My holy name I support. You embarrass me, now prove my name true holy will I. Those countries, they know I true holy will they, how? Prove will I. Israel people I gather, #ALL country I gather, bring-you here home. Clean water I wash-you, dirt remove, your idols destroy will I. Heart new, spirit new I give you—old heart hard I remove, new heart exchange. My spirit I give-you, my law you follow will. Here land you live forever; you become my people, I become your God.'"

Word his Lord.

RESPONSORIAL PSALM (Psalm 42:3, 5; 43:3–4)

(Option A: when Baptism is celebrated)

Deer thirst water, same compare my soul thirst God.

My soul thirst-for God / I go-to-him, his face see, when?

Group, I join-in / group-go there temple
We happy, shout thank-you / people hordes celebrate.

Lord, your light, faithfulness, give-me / lead me
Your holy mountain I arrive / your home enter.

God his altar I go-to (cl:1) / he give-me happy, satisfied
Finish, I sing thank-you / God, my God.

(Option B: when Baptism is not celebrated) (Isaiah 12:2–3, 4, 5–6)
(found after the fifth reading)

(Option C: when Baptism is not celebrated) (Psalm 51:12–13, 14–15, 18–19)

Lord, heart clean, holy, give-me.

God, please heart clean give-me / spirit strong inspire me
Please reject-me not / your Holy Spirit take-out-of-me not.

Give-me happy, save me / a spirit willing give-me
Sinners, I teach-them your way / they connect-to-God will.

Sacrifice, you enjoy not / suppose animal I kill, burn-up, you thumbs-down
My spirit humble I sacrifice / heart humble, sorry, you accept.

LETTER OF PAUL TO THE ROMANS (6:3–11)

Brother~sister, we baptized, show we connect Christ Jesus. We finish die same-as-him. During baptize, we die, bury with Jesus, same-as-him. Jesus, Father raise-up live again, same new life he give us. Suppose we die connect Christ, resurrect connect-him will. We know-that our old sinner body finish die with Jesus there cross; means we fascinate, habit sin finish. Suppose man die, he sin again can't. Suppose we die with Christ, we believe live again with him will. We know-that Jesus once die, resurrect, finish; again die never. Death defeat-him not. He die once for sin destroy; now he lives for God. Same must you think yourselves dead for sin, live for God.

Word his Lord.

GOSPEL ACCLAMATION

(Psalm 118:1–2, 16–17, 22–23)

Alleluia, alleluia, alleluia!

Thank-you Lord, himself good / his mercy continue forever.
People there Israel say quote, / "His mercy continue forever."

Lord himself action mighty / Lord his strong we honor.
I die never, live will I / Lord his action I announce.

Stone people reject / now itself most important support.
God his plan now satisfy / we see, wow, wonderful!

HOLY GOSPEL ACCORDING TO MATTHEW

(28:1–10)

<u>Sabbath</u> finish, first day of week sunrise, <u>Mary Magdalene</u> with other woman, two-of-them go (cl:V) tomb (sign "bury"). Happen earthquake, angel fly-down, stone roll-away, sit-on. Angel look-like lightning-flash, clothes shining. Soldier shock, fall down same dead. Angel inform women, quote, "Fear not. I know Jesus you search-for, but he not here. He finish rise, same he promise. Come, see place past body lay, now gone. Quick inform disciples: 'Jesus finish resurrect, go <u>Galilee</u>, meet-you there.'" Two-of-them leave, happy, afraid. Wrong, Jesus (cl:1) meet-them (cl:V), said, "Peace!" Women kneel, bow, honor. Jesus said, "Hey, fear none. Go, my brothers inform-them they go <u>Galilee</u> must, see me there."

Gospel his Lord.

EASTER SUNDAY

ACTS OF THE APOSTLES

(10:34, 37–43)

<u>Peter</u> tell people, "You finish know story rumor about Jesus, start there <u>Galilee</u> baptism, Holy Spirit and power God give-him. Jesus travel-around, good work++; those people have devil influence-them, heal. God accompany-him. We finish see Jesus #do-do there Jerusalem. Last, Jews kill him, crucify. But third day God raise-him live again, people see-him—but not #ALL. God choose witness few, who? We apostles. Jesus die, resurrect finish, we eat with him. He order us preach #ALL people—preach what? God choose Jesus for judge #ALL people, alive, dead, both. Up-to-now prophets preach about Jesus: suppose you believe him, your sin God forgive.

Word his Lord.

RESPONSORIAL PSALM

(118:1–2, 16–17, 22–23)

Today Lord make special, we happy celebrate.

Thank-you Lord, himself good, / his mercy continue forever
People there Israel say quote, / "His mercy continue forever."

Lord himself action mighty / Lord his strong we honor
I die not, live will I / work his Lord I announce.

Rock, that-one people reject / itself now most important support
Lord his plan now satisfy / we see, wow, true wonderful.

LETTER OF PAUL TO THE COLOSSIANS

(3:1–4)

You finish resurrect with Christ. Now, focus heaven things, there Christ with God. Cherish things connect heaven more-than things connect earth. Die finish you! Your life now secret hide with Christ and God. Happen Christ show-up, you with him full glory will.

Word his Lord.

or

FIRST LETTER OF PAUL TO THE CORINTHIANS (5:6b–8)

You know <u>yeast</u>? Bread make, <u>yeast</u> put-in, knead (mime), increase-in-size. Now, old <u>yeast</u> throw-out, make bread new, clean. Christ finish sacrifice himself. Now we celebrate, old bread compare sin, throw out; new bread compare honest, celebrate.

Word his Lord.

GOSPEL ACCLAMATION

Alleluia

Christ, himself our Lamb, kill~sacrifice
Now we celebrate with Lord.

HOLY GOSPEL ACCORDING TO JOHN (20:1–9)

Early morning first day week, still dark, <u>Mary Magdalene</u> arrive grave, see rock roll-away, gulp; run tell <u>Simon Peter</u> and other disciple, that-one best-friend Jesus, "Lord body, someone steal, put where, I don't-know." Two-of-them (cl:V) go-to grave. Second, he run, arrive first. Enter, shhh. Look-in, see cloth wrap left ground. <u>Peter</u> arrive, enter, see cloth there ground, other cloth wrap-around head, separate, left-there. Now second disciple enter, see, believe! Remember, prophecy about Jesus die, resurrect, two-of-them understand not-yet.

Gospel his Lord.

Second Sunday of Easter DIVINE MERCY SUNDAY

ACTS OF THE APOSTLES
(2:42–47)

Apostles teach, people faithful pay-attention, socialize bread (communion) share, pray together. Apostles, whew! Many wonderful work happen++, people see, surprise, wonder. Everything, believers share; their things sell, money receive, share-around. Every-day group-go temple—plus, in home together bread (communion) share. They happy feast together, praise God. Other people see, respect-them. Every day Lord influence more people connect++, saved.

Word his Lord.

RESPONSORIAL PSALM
(118:2–4, 13–15, 22–24)

Thank Lord, himself good, his love continue forever.

Israel people say / God mercy continue forever.
Priest #ALL say / God mercy continue forever.
People they honor Lord say / God mercy continue forever.

I struggle, fail / but Lord help-me.
Courage, strong Lord give-me / he save me succeed.
Happy celebrate / there tent good people theirs.

Rock, people up-to-now reject / itself become most important support.
Lord his plan now satisfy, / we see, wow, true wonderful.
Today Lord make special / we happy, celebrate.

FIRST LETTER OF PETER
(1:3–9)

Praise God, himself Father his Lord Jesus Christ. He mercy-us, new life, new hope give-us, how? Jesus he die, resurrect live again. Future give-me wonderful things, themselves wear-out never. Where? There heaven. You have faith, means God protect you, save you future last day. Celebrate! Maybe you suffer troubles various must you—why?

Well, your faith important more-than pure gold. Difficult happen++ test, prove your faith strong, cause-you give praise, glory, honor time Jesus Christ come again. You see Jesus not-yet, no-matter, you love him, believe him. You experience happy whew! because you succeed goal—what? <u>Salvation</u> (fingerspell, if time).

Word his Lord.

GOSPEL ACCLAMATION

Alleluia

You believe me, why? You finish see me.
Bless those people see me not-yet, no-matter, believe.

HOLY GOSPEL ACCORDING TO JOHN (20:19–31)

Week, first day, night, disciples assemble room, door locked why? Afraid Jew leaders. Jesus show-up, said, "Peace I give-you." Finish, hands, feet, side, Jesus show. Disciples happy see-him. (Jesus) "Peace I give-you. Father finish send me; now my-turn I send you." Jesus inhale, spread-out-from-mouth, said, "Give-you Holy Spirit. Suppose people sin you forgive, sin dissolve. Suppose you forgive refuse, sin stay."

Happen one apostle name <u>Thomas</u> [that name means twin], he not there. Other disciples inform-him, "Lord we finish see!" He skeptical! "Happen I myself touch Jesus, his hands (point to nail marks), his side slit-open, touch-it, believe will I."

Next-week, again disciples assemble room, also <u>Thomas</u> with, door locked. Jesus show-up, said, "Peace." Look around, there <u>Thomas</u>, beckon, "My hands touch; side, touch. Skeptical, push-aside; now believe!" (Thomas) "My Lord, my God." (Jesus) "You believe now, why? you see me. Bless those people they see me not-yet but still believe." Jesus action many wonderful works, jot-down #ALL shhh, but disciples see. Recent few (on fingers) jot-down for-for? help-you believe Jesus true Messiah, Son his God. You faith have, live forever.

Gospel his Lord.

THIRD SUNDAY OF EASTER

ACTS OF THE APOSTLES

(2:14, 22–33)

[Day Pentecost] <u>Peter</u>, with disciples eleven, inform people audience, quote, "You Jew people, #ALL you live here Jerusalem, you Israel people, pay-attention-me. Jesus, God sent-you-proof what? Jesus action many wonderful happen++. God work through Jesus, you know-that. God plan for sinners take (Jesus), put-up (on cross), crucify, die. But no-matter, God raise-him-up, resurrect live again. Die continue, impossible. Long-ago, <u>David</u> write about Jesus, quote, "Lord I see always with me. He near, I fear none. I happy, celebrate. My body live continue hope; my soul, you abandon dead not, you allow faithful person dissolve not. Right way live, you show-me, happy face-to-face God you inspire."

You know-that long-ago <u>David</u> die, bury, <u>tomb</u> itself still establish up-to-now. <u>David</u> himself prophet. God promise-him his (David's) descendent take-up control will. So, he (David) predict, story about Jesus, himself (Jesus) die, resurrect, his body abandoned, dissolve never. God finish raise-up Jesus, we finish see. Now Jesus there heaven with Father. God promise Holy Spirit give-him, he receive, pour-out (cause).

Word his Lord.

RESPONSORIAL PSALM

(16:1–2, 5, 7–8, 9–10, 11a)

Lord, please, way-to life show-me.

Please care-for me, Lord, you I trust / I say, "You my Lord."
You my food, my drink / my future you control.

I honor Lord why? He advise-me, / during all-night
he teach-my-heart
I continue look-at Lord. / Suppose he near, none bother me.

My heart happy, my soul celebrate / my body confident
Why? My soul you abandon not / my body dissolve, you protect.
Way-to life you show-me / happy face-to-face-you / happy with you
forever.

FIRST LETTER OF PETER (1:17–21)

Each person his actions, Father judge. Mean what? Action right
during life here earth must you. Know-that God save you, how?
Tradition hand-down? No. Gold, silver pay? No. Christ his cherish
blood save you. That blood from quote "Lamb" perfect, holy. Before
world set-up, before, God chose Jesus for-for? Save you. Through
Jesus, you believe God, he God raise-up Jesus, give-him glory. Now,
your faith, hope focus God.

Word his Lord.

GOSPEL ACCLAMATION

Alleluia

Lord Jesus, please teach-us your Bible understand
Cause-my heart fire, excited learn your little-story.

HOLY GOSPEL ACCORDING TO LUKE (24:13–35)

Happen first day week, disciples two walk (cl:V) there town name
<u>Emmaus</u>—there, Jerusalem almost-nothing 7 miles. Two-of-them
discuss recent happen++. Wrong, Jesus approach (cl:1 from left),
walk with (cl:1, V). Two-of-them recognize-him not. (Jesus) "You-
two discuss what?" (Disciples) Shock. One, his name <u>Cleopas</u>, said,
"You don't-know happen++ there Jerusalem few days up-to-now??"
(Jesus) "What happen++?" (Disciples) "Oh, Jesus from <u>Nazareth</u>,
himself prophet expert lecture, work++. Our priest-most sent Jesus
crucify, die. Disappoint. We thought, hoped Jesus will cause Israel free.
Now, three-days up-to-now, women few inform-us strange story.

Today early-morning, women go-to tomb, body gone! They story envision angel tell-them Jesus live again. Men few go-to (tomb), see++—true~work, body gone."

Jesus said, "Pea-brain, you! Prophets write, you believe not-yet. You don't-know Messiah must suffer these-things (on fingers), finish, glory touch can?" Jesus begin Bible explain++ beginning-to-end how connect-to himself. Three-of-them near town, time sunset. Those-two invite Jesus eat with. Jesus accept. Three-of-them enter, sit-down, ready eat. Bread, Jesus bless, break, give-them. Quick, those-two recognize him; wrong, Jesus disappear. Those-two look-at-each-other, said, quote, "Our heart inspire recent he walk with us, Bible explain." Two-of-them stood up, #BACK Jerusalem, room believers assembled enter. Believers inform two-of-them, "True, Lord finish resurrect. Simon see-him true!" Those-two story their experience recent walk road, how Jesus bread break, give-out, succeed recognize-him.

Gospel his Lord.

Fourth Sunday of Easter

ACTS OF THE APOSTLES

(2:14, 36–41)

[Day Pentecost,] Peter, with disciples eleven, inform people audience, quote, "#ALL people its Israel must know true what? Jesus, that-one you crucified, God cause-him become Lord and Messiah." People hear, gulp, "Hey! We #do-do?" (Peter) "Your life change, accept baptize name Jesus Christ. Sin forgive finish, Holy Spirit God-give-you will. God promise you, your children and many people distant-future, Holy Spirit give." Peter continue preach++, said, "Those sinners, defend yourself (from them) must." Many people believe, accept baptize; same day about 3,000 people connect.

Word his Lord.

RESPONSORIAL PSALM

(23:1–3a, 3b–4, 5, 6)

Lord, himself my care-er, give-me everything I need.

Lord, he my care-er, give-me everything I need / there grass area, he give me rest;
Near quiet river, he lead me; / my soul he inspire.

Right way he lead-me for his name honor
Suppose dark valley I walk (cl:1), / doesn't matter, afraid nothing.

He here with-me, accompany, full power, might / courage give-me.

Banquet he prepare, my enemies look-at-me / my head he anoint; my cup (lh) fill-up-overflow.

God good, kind, touch my life / die, I live there his home for ever and ever.

FIRST LETTER OF PETER (2:20–25)

Suppose you patient suffer because you action right, God see, accept. Christ finish suffer for you—why? give example, you suffer same must. Christ sin none, lie nothing. Happen they insult-him, he "gotcha" not. Happen they abuse him, he get-even not. No, he trust God judge-them right. Our sin, Jesus gather-up in his body, bring there cross, die—why? Sin push-aside, live right, can we. His suffer cause-you healed. Before, you lost same compare sheep, but now you have shepherd, your soul he care-for.

Word his Lord.

GOSPEL ACCLAMATION

Alleluia

Lord says, Myself good shepherd
My sheep I know, and they know me.

HOLY GOSPEL ACCORDING TO JOHN (10:1–10)

Jesus said, "True I inform you, any person enter sheep-fence—not gate; other, climb-over fence—that person stealer. Shepherd, he gate-open, walk through (cl:V-legs). Keeper, he open gate, invite (shepherd). His voice sheep hear, each their name summon. #ALL sheep his assemble, shepherd walk away (cl:1), sheep flock-after— why? his voice they know. Suppose they sheep don't-know who summon them, follow refuse because his voice they don't-know."

Jesus story++, but apostles past-their-ears, understand none. Jesus explain, "I myself compare sheep gate. #ALL other up-to-now compare stealers. Sheep follow-them not. I (hon) true gate. Happen I open-gate, person (cl:1) walk toward-me, he safe, defend. He can out, in, out, in, eat, enjoy. Stealer come for-for? Steal, kill, destroy. But I come for give life plenty."

Gospel his Lord.

FIFTH SUNDAY OF EASTER

ACTS OF THE APOSTLES   (6:1–7)

People more, more become disciples, connect; wrong, that group
Greek complain—why? <u>Widows</u> theirs (Greek) food reduce; <u>widows</u>
theirs Jew, food-exceed!—equal not. Apostles twelve summon,
come-here, meeting, said, "Word his God we ignore, push aside,
busy serve, food share-around—not right. Better yourselves choose++
men seven, themselves strong pray, holy; we ordain them become
servers. Finish, we concentrate pray, preach word God can." #ALL
accept, pick++ who? (1) <u>Stephen</u>, himself inspire faith and Holy
Spirit, (2) <u>Philip</u>, (3) <u>Prochorus</u>, (4) <u>Nicanor</u>, (5) <u>Timon</u>, (6) <u>Parmenes</u>,
and (7) <u>Nicolaus</u>, himself finish become Jew. Seven men there,
apostles face-to-face, they (apostles) pray, ordain. Word his God
continue spread. Many people there Jerusalem become disciples, also
many Jew priest become Christian.

Word his Lord.

RESPONSORIAL PSALM   (33:1–2, 4–5, 18–19)

Lord, mercy-me, you we trust.

You good people, celebrate Lord / people honest praise-him,
appropriate.
Thank-him Lord sing / praise-him sign-ASL.

Word his Lord itself right / his work we trust can.
He love judge~fair, right / Lord his kindness spread earth.

Lord, he care-for those honor-him / he mercy-them, they hope.
Die, he save-them / food blow-on-hand, he feed-them.

Lord himself compare stone. Men reject (him), but God see, cherish. You same compare stone, God put++, become what? Holy group priest, yourselves sacrifice-to God, he accept through Jesus Christ. Bible says, quote, "See, foundation stone I establish—means Jesus— itself important stone. Who trust, courage will." Stone true important #IF faith have. Suppose faith none, it stone compare, quote, "stone builders put-aside, now become important support." Stone, some people will trip, fall—how? Believe God his word refuse. Fault-self. But God choose you become king priest, holy group, people connect-him, for announce his glory work. Dark (l), he summon-you enter wonderful light (r).

Word his Lord.

GOSPEL ACCLAMATION

Alleluia

Myself way, truth, life, Lord says
See Father want? Must through me.

HOLY GOSPEL ACCORDING TO JOHN (14:1–12)

Disciples, Jesus tell-them, quote, "Worry, no-wave. You trust God, same trust me must. My Father his house have many rooms. Now I inform-you, I go place prepare for you. True, I go, place prepare; ready, come #BACK, bring-you-there. Why? You continue live connect-me. That place, you already know how touch." Thomas said, "Lord, you go where, we don't-know—find way how?" (Jesus) "I myself true way, and honest, and life. Touch Father want? Through me (hon) must. Philip said, "Lord, Father show-us, satisfied will." (Jesus) "Up-to-now, I accompany++, still you don't know me? Who see me (hon), see Father same-as-me. How can you tell me show-you Father? Father, me, united same, skeptical you?? I preach, my idea, shhh. Father live in me, he work through me. Believe true Father, me, two-of-us connect. <u>Or</u>, believe because work I succeed. I promise, any person have faith me, he succeed work same-as-me, and more. Why? Because I depart, go-to Father."

Gospel his Lord.

Sixth Sunday of Easter

ACTS OF THE APOSTLES

(8:5–8, 14–17)

Town name <u>Samaria</u>, apostle name <u>Philip</u> travel, preach about Jesus. People #ALL listen-with-eyes, <u>Philip</u> wonderful work, they see, fascinated. Many people their body have spirit bad; wrong, spirit out, scream. Other people, body freeze, also several crippled, they healed. People #ALL happy, celebrate, whew! Apostles there Jerusalem hear rumor what? People there <u>Samaria</u> finish accept word his God, so <u>Peter</u> and <u>John</u> send. Two-of-them go (cl:V), pray Holy Spirit touch those people. Understand, those people finish baptize name Lord Jesus, but Holy Spirit touch not-yet. Two-of-them ordain++, Holy Spirit inspire.

Word his Lord.

RESPONSORIAL PSALM

(66:1–3, 4–5, 6–7, 16, 20)

#ALL people shout, happy sign-ASL.

#ALL people shout happy sign-ASL / sing glory, praise his holy name.
His wonderful praise announce / God his actions wonderful.

People all-over earth worship, sing praise / your name sign-ASL praise.
Come, see God his work / his wonderful action for #ALL people.

Ocean, he change dry land / river separate, they walk across.
Now we celebrate God / his power control forever.

#ALL you honor God, pay-attention-me / he #do-do for me, I story.
Bless God, he refuse me not / I pray, he kind give-me.

FIRST LETTER OF PETER (3:15–18)

Honor Lord Jesus in heart. Suppose someone ask-you why you trust God, halt (raised open hand), ready answer quiet, respect. Live right way, why? Suppose someone criticize you, later he see your life good, Christian, pull-in-head will he. Suppose God wants you suffer, well, suffer for actions good better than suffer for actions bad. Jesus suffer, die once for #ALL. Jesus Himself sin none, die for sinners—why? Want lead-you there God. Jesus his body die, but spirit live continue.

Word his Lord.

GOSPEL ACCLAMATION

Alleluia

Lord says, Any person love me, my word he obey.
Finish, my Father love him, two-of-us inspire him.

HOLY GOSPEL ACCORDING TO JOHN (14:15–21)

Apostles, Jesus tell-them, "Suppose you love me, my command obey must. Pray Father will I, other helper he give you continue with you forever—who? Spirit of honest. Spirit, world accept not—why? See can't (^), understand can't (^). You different. You understand because spirit touch you, inspire you. I abandon-you alone not; #BACK will I. Soon, near-future, I leave, world see me none. But you see me, know-that I live continue, and you live-continue, same-as-me. Future, you know-that I connect Father, and you, I connect++. Any person obey my command, that person love me; person love me, my Father love him, and I love him and show-him myself (hon).

Gospel his Lord.

ASCENSION OF THE LORD

ACTS OF THE APOSTLES

My first letter explain everything Jesus action, teach up-to-now, until day Jesus ascend heaven. First, apostles Jesus choose++, understand, Holy Spirit help-him; finish, teach-them++. Jesus suffer, die, resurrect; finish, prove himself still alive. How? During 40 days, Jesus show-up from-time-to-time, story about kingdom his God. One time, Jesus tell-them "Jerusalem stay, wait Father his promise true happen. Past, John, he baptize water, but near-future few days Holy Spirit inspire-you."

Apostles question-him, "Lord, Israel promote-to-thumb, control take-up now?" Jesus answer, "Exact time, don't-know. Father himself know. Happen Holy Spirit influence-you, you strong will; finish, preach about me here Jerusalem, [there Judea and Samaria] all-over earth must you." Finish, Jesus ascend~dissolve.

They continue look-up; wrong, men two, clothes white, tap-on-shoulder, "You stand, look-up, for-for? Jesus, himself recent ascend, #BACK will."

Word his Lord.

RESPONSORIAL PSALM

(47:2–3, 6–7, 8–9)

God take~control, we shout happy, blow-horn loud for God.

You people, celebrate / shout happy for God.
Lord most high, wonderful / himself king control earth.

God take~control, people shout happy / blow-horn loud for Lord.
Praise sing for God, sign-ASL / praise sing for our king, sign-ASL.

God himself king control earth / praise sing, sign-ASL.
#ALL countries God control / holy throne God sit.

LETTER OF PAUL TO THE EPHESIANS

(1:17–23)

God and Lord Jesus Christ true glory. Please he give-you spirit wise, oh-I-see, help-you know him clear. Please he help-you understand (1) wonderful hope he offer-you, (2) glory he give-you share, (3) his power whew! in us believers. Same power God use raise-up Christ, put-him-on-right sit there heaven, every controller and angel exceed, every name now and future exceed. Everything God put under Christ control; himself compare head, church compare body. Jesus his body spread, touch whole world.

Word his Lord.

GOSPEL ACCLAMATION

Alleluia

Lord says, #ALL countries go-to, teach;
Myself accompany-you always, until world collapse, dissolve.

HOLY GOSPEL ACCORDING TO MATTHEW

(28:16–20)

Disciples eleven group-go there <u>Galilee</u>, mountain same Jesus tell them go-to. Notice Jesus, their doubt dissolve, kneel-down, worship. Jesus come forward (cl:1), said, quote, "God finish give-me full authority there heaven, here earth both. Go, preach #ALL people, baptize them name Father, Son, Holy Spirit. Everything I finish tell-you, teach-them. Know-that I continue accompany-you always, until world collapse~dissolve, blow-off-hand.

Gospel his Lord.

SEVENTH SUNDAY OF EASTER

ACTS OF THE APOSTLES

(1:12–14)

Jesus ascend finish, apostles #BACK Jerusalem, not far, almost-nothing, one day travel. Arrive, go room upstairs, other apostles there: Peter, John, James, Andrew, Philip, Thomas, Bartholomew, Matthew, James, Simon, and other Judas. #ALL together pray++ continue. Also have women few, plus Mary and Jesus his brothers.

Word his Lord.

RESPONSORIAL PSALM

(27:1, 4, 7–8)

I believe good things Lord give-me during my life.

Lord, himself give-me light, save me / I fear who?
Lord, himself protect me / I dread who?

Only thing I ask from Lord, what? / Live with him his house forever
His beauty look-at++ / his heaven think-about++

Lord, my cry-out pay-attention / pity-me, answer-me
You, my heart hungers / you, my eyes search-for.

FIRST LETTER OF PETER

(4:13–16)

Christ his suffer you share? Celebrate! Happen his glory he show-you, happy will you. Suppose people insult you because yourself Christian, means God his Spirit full glory touch you. Understand, suppose you suffer because you kill, steal, action bad things, other person his rights ruin, #TB. Those-things (on fingers) you must not. But, suppose you suffer because yourself Christian, ashamed not. Better, glory give God—why? Yourself follow Christ true.

Word his Lord.

GOSPEL ACCLAMATION

Alleluia

Lord says, I abandon-you alone, depart, never;
#BACK will I, your heart celebrate.

HOLY GOSPEL ACCORDING TO JOHN (17:1–11)

Heaven Jesus look-up, said, quote, "Father, right time pah! now.
Glory give-me your Son; finish, glory your Son give-you. Authority
over #ALL people you give-me—why? Eternal life give-them can I.
Eternal life means what? Means know you, only true God, and know
Jesus Christ, that-one you finish send. Glory here earth I finish give-
you—how? Work you give-me, I complete pah! Now, Father, please
glory give-me, same glory I have with you long-ago before world set-
up. Those people you give-me, your name I teach-them. They true
your people—why? Your command they obey. Now they understand:
everything I have, you give-me. Story you inform-me, I inform-them,
they accept. They know true I come from you; they believe you
finish send-me.

I pray for them—not for whole world, no, only for these people you
give-me, why? they true your people. Everything mine, true yours.
Everything yours true mine same-as-you. My glory they show. World
I stay not; but they stay, I go-to you."

Gospel his Lord.

Pentecost Sunday

ACTS OF THE APOSTLES

(2:1–11)

Happen day <u>Pentecost</u>, believers assemble together. Wrong happen, loud-noise compare wind-strong-blow—look-at-each-other, afraid. Surprise, show-up fire, separate, each person fire-over-head++ (cl:1, 4=fire). Holy Spirit inspire #ALL, begin lecture language different++ same Holy Spirit order-them.

Same-time there Jerusalem, Jew people from country different++ assembled. Noise they hear, all-eyes look (cl:4,4), puzzled—why? Each hear apostles speak language his++. Shock! Said, "Hey, they from <u>Galilee</u>, right? How happen we hear language his++, my, how? We come here from many different countries: [<u>Judea</u>, <u>Pontus</u>, <u>Asia</u>, Egypt, <u>Libya</u>,] area, also visitors from Rome—#ALL themselves Jew <u>or</u> connect Jew religion. Each one hear them preach his++ language about God wonderful success.

Word his Lord.

RESPONSORIAL PSALM

(104:1, 24, 29–30, 31, 34)

Lord, your spirit send-down, all-over earth become new.

My soul honor Lord / God, yourself wonderful true.
Many things God make+++ / earth hordes he make.

Suppose breathe, you stop-it / they die, dissolve.
Happen your spirit touch, they live / all-over earth become new.

Lord his glory continue forever / Lord make++, satisfy.
My song, Lord enjoy / I happy connect-to-him.

FIRST LETTER OF PAUL TO THE CORINTHIANS (12:3b–7, 12–13)

You say, quote, "Jesus true Lord," how possible? Holy Spirit inspire-you. Have skill many various, but Spirit one; have ministry many various, but Lord one; have work many various, but God one, himself succeed everything. Each person have Holy Spirit inside for benefit #ALL same-around. Body itself one; hands, arms, feet, various have; no-matter, still body one. Christ compare same. #ALL people, no matter Jew, Greek, slave, free, no-matter, #ALL baptize become united-around quote "body" group one—how? Holy Spirit influence.

Word his Lord.

GOSPEL ACCLAMATION

Alleluia

Come, Holy Spirit, our heart touch,
Your love inspire.

HOLY GOSPEL ACCORDING TO JOHN (20:19–23)

New week, first day, evening, disciples meet room, close-door, lock—why? Afraid Jews. Wrong, Jesus show-up, said, "Peace you." Hands (nail-prints), side (cut) show-them. Disciples look-at-Jesus, happy, celebrate. (Jesus) "Peace, calm-down. Father finish send-me, now my-turn send you same." Jesus breathe, exhale-on-them, said, "Holy Spirit I-give-you. Suppose man sin, you forgive, I forgive succeed. Suppose you forgive-him refuse, his sin stay."

Gospel his Lord.

HOLY TRINITY

BOOK OF EXODUS

(34:4–6, 8–9)

Early-morning, Moses go-to mountain name <u>Sinai</u>, follow Lord command. Rock two (cl) bring. There cloud, Lord come down (cl:1), meet, announce his name, quote, "<u>Lord</u>." Finish, Lord pass-by (cl:1), shout, "Myself God full mercy, love; slow become angry; kind, faithful, excessive whew!" Quick Moses kneel, bow, worship. Finish, he said, "Lord, suppose you love me, please our group-travel join-in. Those people stubborn true, but please our sin forgive and accept we become your people connect."

RESPONSORIAL PSALM

(Daniel 3:52, 53, 54, 55, 56)

Glory, praise forever.

Honor you, Lord God up-to-now / praise, honor forever.
Honor your holy, glory name / praise, honor forever.

Honor you in your holy temple glory / praise, glory forever.

Honor you there throne your kingdom / praise, honor forever.

You there heaven throne, everything you see / praise, honor forever.

SECOND LETTER OF PAUL TO THE CORINTHIANS

(12:11–13)

Brother++, your life change, improve. Encourage each other. Live harmony, peace, for-for? God, himself full love, peace, connect-you will. Happen meet, holy kiss put-on-each-other's-cheek. Christians here #ALL say hello. Grace from Lord Jesus Christ, love from God, fellowship from Holy Spirit, touch #ALL.

Word his Lord.

GOSPEL ACCLAMATION

Alleluia

Glory give-to Father, Son, Holy Spirit
God himself up-to-now, now, and forever.

HOLY GOSPEL ACCORDING TO JOHN (3:16–18)

Man name <u>Nicodemus</u>, Jesus tell-him, quote, "God love world so-much, his only son he give—for-for? Any person believe son, that person die not: he live forever. Son God send here world for punish people?? No-wave. Save people through son, God want. Suppose person believe Jesus, God punish-him not. But, any person believe not, God punish finish, why? God only son he believe refuse.

Gospel his Lord.

BODY AND BLOOD OF CHRIST

BOOK OF DEUTERONOMY

Moses tell people, quote, "Remember, 40 years up-to-now, Lord your God lead you across desert—why? Test, let's-see you willing his command obey. God allow-you suffer hunger; finish, give-you <u>manna</u>, food that-one you know-nothing, your ancestors know-nothing. God want show what? Person eat bread only, survive can't. Require must have word his God for live. Remember Lord your God. Egypt, there you slave, he bring-you out-free. Big, awful desert, it have snake and bug scorpion, he lead you safe; dry, water none, rock, he cause water flow-out-of. <u>Manna</u>, that food your ancestors know-nothing, he feed you.

Word his Lord.

RESPONSORIAL PSALM

(147:12–13, 14–15, 19–20)

Jerusalem, praise Lord, Alleluia!

Jerusalem, glory give-to Lord / #ALL people praise your God
City strong he finish give-you / your children he finish bless.

Country peace he give-you / food wonderful he provide
Earth he command / earth quick obey.

Long-ago his people he inform / his law he teach-them
Other country he cherish not / his law inform-them not-yet, alleluia.

FIRST LETTER OF PAUL TO THE CORINTHIANS

(10:16–17)

Wine we bless, itself blood his Christ, right? Bread we break, itself body his Christ, right? Bread itself one loaf (cl), means we, many people no-matter, we become one body-group—why? We #ALL eat one bread-loaf.

Word his Lord.

GOSPEL ACCLAMATION

Alleluia

Lord says, Myself true bread from heaven
This (hon) bread eat, live forever.

HOLY GOSPEL ACCORDING TO JOHN

(6:51–58)

Jew hordes Jesus inform, quote, "I myself true bread from heaven. Suppose this (hon) bread any person eat, he live forever. Bread I give— what? My body, for life give-to world." People Jew look-at-each-other, discuss, "His body he give-us eat, how?" Jesus said, "I promise you, suppose my body you eat not, my blood drink not, you have life nothing. Suppose person my body eat, my blood drink, he have life forever. Happen last day, I raise-him live again. Understand, my body true~work eat can; my blood true~work drink can. Any person eat my body, drink my blood, two-of-us connect. Father himself have life. He send me, and I live because connect-God. Same-as person my body eat, he live because connect-me. This (hon) bread come-down from heaven. Manna, your ancestors eat, die no-matter. Suppose any person this (hon) bread eat, he live forever."

Gospel his Lord.

Second Sunday in Ordinary Time

BOOK OF THE PROPHET ISAIAH (49:3, 5–6)

Lord finish tell-me, "Israel, you my servant true. My glory, you show."
Lord himself make me for-for? Serve him, his people Israel gather,
bring-them home heaven. Glory, Lord give-me; strong he give-me.
Lord tell-me, "You serve me, my people gather, bring-them-here
home—trivial; not enough. Promote you will I, you become compare
light for #ALL people; people far-away, no-matter, they know-that
I save them."

Word his Lord.

RESPONSORIAL PSALM (40:2, 4, 7–8, 8–9, 10)

Here I (hon), you want I willing obey.

I up-to-now wait-for Lord / he look-at me, pay-attention-me
New song he give-me / sign-ASL for Lord.

Animal sacrifice you don't-want / but I pay-attention, obey, you want
Animal kill, burn, you don't-want / I say, "Myself offer-to-you."

Bible write, inform-me #do-do
You law I cherish-in-heart.

Your judge~fair I announce / face-to-face people hordes
I restrain-myself not / Lord, you know-that.

FIRST LETTER OF PAUL TO THE CORINTHIANS (1:1–3)

Myself <u>Paul</u>, God summon-me become apostle his; brother <u>Sosthenes</u>,
two-of-us write-to you church there <u>Corinth</u>. You finish accept Jesus,
become holy, #ALL people themselves trust, honor Jesus Christ, you

connect. Grace and peace from God Father and Lord Jesus Christ touch-you.

Word his Lord.

GOSPEL ACCLAMATION

Alleluia

God his son became man, live here with us.
Any person accept him, he give-them power become children his God.

HOLY GOSPEL ACCORDING TO JOHN   (1:29–34)

Jesus come (cl:1), <u>Joh</u>n Baptist see, said, quote, "There Lamb <u>of</u> God, sin world he forgive. Past, I preach other man will come, himself important than me. That-one he. I know him not-yet, but people I baptize (immerse) in water for-for? Inform about him." <u>Joh</u>n preach more, say, "I finish see spirit from heaven flutter-down, touch-him. I puzzled, but God inform-me what? Happen I see spirit flutter down, touch—that-one will send Holy Spirit. Now I know-that he himself true~work son his God."

Gospel his Lord.

THIRD SUNDAY IN ORDINARY TIME

BOOK OF THE PROPHET ISAIAH

(8:23—9:3)

First, land name <u>Zebulun</u> and <u>Naphtali</u>, Lord demote-to-baby-finger; but now there land near <u>Jordan</u> river—non-Jews live there—glory he give. Suffering gone, dark dissolve, sad blow-off-hand. People past live dark, now see bright-light; past live land obscure, now Lord light-shine-down. God give-them happy, celebrate. They celebrate face-to-face-God same harvest time, excited money share-around. Why? Their burden, their suffering, God destroy same long-ago, [there <u>Midian</u>].

Word his Lord.

RESPONSORIAL PSALM

(27:1–4, 13–14)

Lord himself give-me light, save-me

Lord himself give-me light, save me / who I fear, who?
Lord himself protect my life / dread nothing.

Only-one thing I pray-to Lord / only-one I want, what?
Lord, his house live with / forever and ever
Lord, his beauty look-at++ / his temple see.

I believe Lord will bless me / now, during my life
Patient wait-for Lord, brave / stand-strong, wait for Lord.

FIRST LETTER OF PAUL TO THE CORINTHIANS

(1:10–13, 17)

Brother, sister, I pray, please everything agree, argue not, purpose united. Gossip I hear, what? You up-to-now argue, disagree. Some say, "<u>Paul</u>, I connect." Other say, "<u>Cephas</u>, I connect" or "<u>Apollos</u>" or "Christ, I connect." ? Christ himself divided? Paul die for you? You baptize connect <u>Paul</u>? No!

Christ send-me for-for? Gospel preach. Expert lecture he give-me not, why? Cross itself most important.

Word his Lord.

GOSPEL ACCLAMATION

Alleluia

Gospel heaven, Jesus announce
People their sick, he heal.

HOLY GOSPEL ACCORDING TO MATTHEW (4:12–23)

John Baptist arrest, throw jail. Gossip Jesus hear, decide there Galilee go-to. Area Zebulun and Naphtali he touch—that-one prophet Isaiah long-ago write, quote, "But now there land near Jordan river, non-Jews live there, glory he give-it. Suffering gone, dark dissolve, sad blow-off-hand. People past live dark, now see bright-light; past live land obscure, now Lord light-shine-down." Jesus preach, say, quote, "Your life change. Heaven kingdom near-future come."

One day, near ocean, Jesus walk, see brothers two, Simon [later name change Peter] and Andrew. Two-of-them work fish catch-in-net. Jesus tell them, "Come with me. From-now-on, people catch-in-net." Quick, two-of-them drop-net, follow. Three-of-them walk (cl:3), see brothers two name James and John. Two-of-them with father sit boat, net fix. Jesus summon-them; quick, two-of-them father left-there, follow.

Galilee Jesus travel-around, teach, gospel announce, those people sick heal.

Gospel his Lord.

FOURTH SUNDAY IN ORDINARY TIME

BOOK OF THE PROPHET ZEPHANIAH

(2:3, 3:12–13)

#ALL you people humble, God law you obey? Search-for Lord, other people judge fair, self become humble—why? Happen Lord angry, you safe. Small group left-there will I, people themselves humble, faithful, trust Lord—those people who? Israel. They action wrong none; lie none, flatter none. Their sheep they care-for, who pick-on-them? none.

Word his Lord.

RESPONSORIAL PSALM

(146:6–7, 8–9, 9–10)

Happy those people poor spirit, God his kingdom belong-to them

Lord himself faithful forever / people oppressed, he judge fair
People hungry, he feed / people prison, out free.

Blind, Lord give-them see / suffer, Lord support
People honest, Lord love / know~new~person, Lord protect.

They have father none, husband none, Lord care-for /
but those bad, their way Lord mess-up.
Lord control forever / your God control forever, alleluia.

FIRST LETTER OF PAUL TO THE CORINTHIANS

(1:26–31)

Think, look-back time God first summon-you. Past, you wise not, powerful not, rich not. People pea-brain God choose++— why? People wise, give-them shock. Weak he choose++— why? People strong, give-them shock. People humble, trivial he choose++—why? People arrogant, give-them shock. Face-to-face Lord, brag impossible. But you, Christ Jesus, connect. His wise he give-you. He cause-you holy, bless, save. Brag you want? Brag about Lord.

Word his Lord.

GOSPEL ACCLAMATION

Alleluia

Celebrate happy, why?
There heaven God give-you wonderful.

HOLY GOSPEL ACCORDING TO MATTHEW

(5:1–12a)

Jesus see people hordes, mountain walk-up, with disciples sit,
say quote,
"You people depend-on God, bless you, why? Kingdom heaven
he-give-you will.

You people sad, bless you—God kind-to-you.

You humble, bless you—land take-up control will.

You thirst for judge~fair, bless you—satisfy will.

You give mercy, bless you—God mercy-you.

Your heart cherish God, bless you—see God will you.

You bring peace, bless you—name-you children his God.

You live right, hit persecute-you, bless you, why? future you,
heaven, connect.

Suppose you follow me, wrong happen people insult-you, hate-you,
lie~gossip about you, bless you. Celebrate happy—why? There
heaven have wonderful <u>reward</u> give-you."

Gospel his Lord.

FIFTH SUNDAY IN ORDINARY TIME

BOOK OF THE PROPHET ISAIAH

(58:7–10)

Those hungry? your bread share. Those have home none? care-for. Person naked? clothes give-him, ignore-him not. Finish, you shine will; your hurt quick healed; power God give-you, his glory protect you. You pray, he answer will. You call out help-me, he say, "Here I (hon)." Oppress, lie, gossip, throw-out. Hungry? bread give. Weak? help. Finish, dark become bright compare day.

Word his Lord.

RESPONSORIAL PSALM

(112:4–5, 6–7, 8–9)

Dark, no-matter, good person himself compare light for other people see.

Suppose dark, no matter, good person compare light / himself give mercy, judge~fair
Suppose person kind, lend willing, fine-wiggle / his business he action fair.

Person good stand-strong / people look-back, remember him forever
Gossip, he afraid not / he know himself honest, Lord he trust.

His heart stand-strong, fear nothing / people poor, he give-them, help-them
He judge fair forever / glory will he.

FIRST LETTER OF PAUL TO THE CORINTHIANS

(2:1–5)

Happen I first come-here preach, I expert lecture? Not. Wise~wow? Not. I decide come-here, big-brains push-aside, become know-nothing—except Christ, himself crucified. That's-all! I come-here weak, afraid, knees-trembling. I preach, teach how? Smart, wise?

No. Holy Spirit his power I show-you—why? My wise your faith depend-on, no—God his power depend-on.

Word his Lord.

GOSPEL ACCLAMATION

Alleluia

Lord says, Myself light for world
Any person follow me, light I give-him for live.

HOLY GOSPEL ACCORDING TO MATTHEW (5:13–16)

Jesus tell disciples: "You compare salt. Suppose salt taste (mime smacking lips) none, increase taste how? Impossible. Salt itself worthless. Throw-out.

"You compare light for world. Mountain, city establish-on-top, hide impossible. Suppose person strike-match candle, #do-do? Basket put-over-it (mime)? No, shelf, candle put-on, house light-shine. Same you. Your light show must—why? Your good work, people see, oh-I-see, glory give God."

Gospel his Lord.

Sixth Sunday in Ordinary Time

BOOK OF SIRACH

(15:15–20)

You choose. Obey commandments, save you. Trust God, live will. God offer-you fire, water. You prefer which? God give-you. Life (l), death (r); good (l), evil (r), you pick which, point-point, God give-you. Lord himself wise~wow; he powerful, he see everything. God watch-you; your action, he understand. He command-you action wrong? never. He encourage-you sin? never.

Word his Lord.

RESPONSORIAL PSALM

(119:1–2, 4–5, 17–18, 33–34)

Happy people they follow law his Lord.

Happy those people innocent / law his Lord they follow.
Happy those people obey his order / their heart search-for him.

You (God) order-us / your law we obey.
Help-me stubborn~continue / your rules obey.

Mercy-me your servant / I continue live, your word follow.
Cause-me open-eyes / your wonderful law I see can.

Lord, your law teach-me / obey fully can I.
Help-me your law understand / always dwell-on, cherish.

FIRST LETTER OF PAUL TO THE CORINTHIANS

(2:6–10)

Brother~sister, we preach wise for people mature. Now time-period, our wise you follow? No. King himself near-future gone, you follow? No. We preach God his wise, itself strange, secret, long-ago God himself invent for give-us glory. Now king understand nothing—proof what? Lord Jesus, king crucified-him. But Bible write, quote,

"People love God, he (God) prepare for them what? Don't-know . . . we see not-yet, hear not-yet, understand not-yet, what." God his spirit inform-us. Everything, spirit analyze; God himself, spirit analyze.

Word his Lord.

GOSPEL ACCLAMATION

Alleluia

God His word become man, live here earth.
Any person accept him, they become children his God.

HOLY GOSPEL ACCORDING TO MATTHEW (5:17–37)

Jesus tell disciples, quote, "You think I come for law destroy? No, I come for law satisfy. Understand, law itself continue, subtract none, until heaven, earth dissolve. Means what? Any person break commandment or teach other people break commandment, that person become demote-to-baby-finger there heaven. But any person obey and teach commandments, he become promote-to-thumb. I inform-you, those scribes, Pharisees, they holier-than-thou, you people good beat-them (shot-h) must; finish, touch heaven can you.

You hear story, 'Kill not. Any person kill, judge-him must.' I tell-you, any person become angry, tell brother, 'Pea-brain, you,' judge, hell will. So, suppose altar you go-to, ready sacrifice, wrong, thought show-up brother angry-me, suspend, leave-it-there; go-to brother, ask forgive, united, finish, #BACK go-ahead sacrifice. Suppose argue, agree~solve before court touch—why? Your enemy, he complain judger, he judger order throw-you prison. I promise, prison you stuck until pay-off-debt full.

You hear story, 'You adultery not.' I tell-you, any person woman look-at (cl:f,f), lust, himself finish adultery in heart. Suppose your eye cause-you sin, tear-out, throw-away. Lose one eye (l), whole body throw-in hell (r), prefer it (lost eye). Suppose your hand cause-you

104

sin, cut-off, throw-away. Lose one hand (l), whole body throw-in hell (r), prefer it (lost hand).

You hear story, 'Any person divorce, paper give wife must he.' I tell-you, any person divorce—understand, marriage itself follow law—he husband cause-her adultery; and suppose man marry with she woman herself finish divorced, man he adultery.

You hear story, 'False promise, not. #IF you promise, keep must.' I tell-you, promise never. Promise name heaven—no, there God throne. Promise name earth—no, here God control. Promise name Jerusalem—no, there God his city. Promise on yourself—no, you power none. You say Yes, mean Yes. You say No, mean No. More exaggerate, devil urge."

Gospel his Lord.

SEVENTH SUNDAY IN ORDINARY TIME

BOOK OF LEVITICUS
(19:1–2, 17–18)

Moses, Lord tell-him, "Israel people, tell them become holy must you, why? I myself their God, I holy. Brother, sister hate dwell-on, get-even, not. Person he action wrong, you face-to-face, discuss must, but yourself sin not. Hate-him not, revenge not. You love yourself, love other people same. Lord inform-you."

Word his Lord.

RESPONSORIAL PSALM
(103:1–2, 3–4, 8, 10, 12–13)

Lord himself kind, mercy.

My soul honor Lord / his holy name I worship.
My soul honor Lord / his benefit I remember, forget not.

Your sin, he forgives / your sick, he heals.
Your life ruin, he saves / kind, mercy, he gives-you.

Lord himself kind, mercy / angry postpone, kind excessive.
Our sin, he get-even not / our wrong, he punish not.

East, west far-apart / same our sins far-away.
Children, father mercy-them / same God mercy-us.

FIRST LETTER OF PAUL TO THE CORINTHIANS
(3:16–23)

Brother~sister, ? you know-that God his spirit live in-heart?? Means you yourself now become quote "temple." Suppose temple someone destroy, God destroy-him, why? God his temple true holy honorific. Understand clear: you think yourself wise? Better become pea-brain, why? World wise, God see, make-me-sick, it. Bible write, quote, "People wise, plan++, God 'gotcha!'" Also, "People wise, their thought God finish know, it worthless." Please, you boast people there, there, there . . . no. You finish #OWN everything: (1) <u>Paul</u>, (2) <u>Apollos</u>, (3) <u>Cephas</u>, (4) world, (5) life, death (6) now time-period, future time-period—#ALL yours. And you connect who? Christ. And he Christ connect God.

Word his Lord.

GOSPEL ACCLAMATION

Alleluia

Suppose Christ his word you obey,
God his love become perfect in you.

HOLY GOSPEL ACCORDING TO MATTHEW

(5:38–48)

You finish hear story, quote, "You take-my-eye, I take-your-eye. You punch-my-mouth, I punch-your-mouth." I teach different. Get-even not. Suppose someone slap-my-cheek, offer-him (point to other cheek). Suppose someone wants court, force-you shirt give-him, coat give-him both. Suppose someone force-you one <u>mile</u> carry-heavy, willing two <u>mile</u> carry. Suppose someone ask borrow, give, ignore-him not.

You finish hear story, quote, "Friends, love must; enemy hate." I teach different. Enemy, love, pray for him, why? Your Father heaven love him. Sunshine, rain he (God) give for people good, bad, same, equal. Suppose friends you love . . . so-what? Sinners love friends! Suppose friends you chat-with . . . well? #ALL people see friend, hello. You different. Father heaven perfect, same perfect must you.

Gospel his Lord.

EIGHTH SUNDAY IN ORDINARY TIME

BOOK OF THE PROPHET ISAIAH

(49:14–15)

Jerusalem people say, "God abandon-me; he forget me." ? Baby, mother abandon, forget, possible?? Cherish dissolve, possible?? Suppose mother forget, no-matter—I forget you never.

Word his Lord.

RESPONSORIAL PSALM

(62:2–3, 6–7, 8–9)

My soul rest with God only.

Only God give my soul rest / himself save me
Only he my support, my savior / my defender, I fear nothing.

Only God give my soul rest / himself give-me hope
Only he my support, my savior / my defender, I fear nothing.

Only God give me safe, glory / himself give-me strong, protect-me
People, please, always trust-him / your prayer sign-ASL-to-him.

FIRST LETTER OF PAUL TO THE CORINTHIANS

(4:1–5)

Brother~sister: Our duty what? Serve Christ, his gospel teach. Important point: boss, servant faithful obey, follow must. Maybe you look-me-up-and-down, judge me faithful <u>or</u> not . . . don't-mind me. I analyze-heart, judge myself, can't. I feel myself wrong none, but Lord himself decide. So, you look-over-carefully, judge, no-wave. Wait Lord come, bring light. Heart dark, light-shine-on, show clear. Finish, God judge, praise.

Word his Lord.

GOSPEL ACCLAMATION

Alleluia

God his word itself live succeed
Our secret thoughts, he know.

HOLY GOSPEL ACCORDING TO MATTHEW

(6:24–34)

Disciples, Jesus tell-them, "Suppose boss two have, serve both can't. Him (l) love, him (r) hate; or him (r) cherish, him (l) hate. God, money, cherish both can't. Now inform-you, worry about life, eat, drink, clothes, finish! Life cherish, but food so-so. Body cherish, but clothes trivial. Example, birds work, farm, plant, harvest nothing, but food plenty have. How? God give. Same you. Suppose you worry, your life exaggerate can? You worry clothes, finish! Look-at flowers. Work++ nothing, but clothes beautiful they. King clothes fancy, they beat (shot-h). Grass worthless, but beautiful flowers God give-it. You think God don't-care you? Faith little-bit, you. You worry eat what, drink what, clothes what, stop! Your Father heaven knows you need these-things (on fingers). But first enthusiastic God his kingdom, finish, these-things (on fingers) God give-you. Worry tomorrow? No, tomorrow what-shrug. Today have problems enough."

Gospel his Lord.

NINTH SUNDAY IN ORDINARY TIME

BOOK OF DEUTERONOMY
(11:18, 26–28, 32)

People, Moses tell-them, "My teach, you memorize~cherish must. My word, wrap-around-arm, tie-around-head. I offer choice, bless, curse. God his commandments I recent teach-you, you obey? Bless. Obey refuse, ignore-him, false <u>gods</u> follow? Curse. Warn-you, law I recent teach-you, obey!"

Word his Lord.

RESPONSORIAL PSALM
(31:2–3, 3–4, 17, 25)

Lord, yourself my rock, my savior.

Lord, please protect me / allow me shame never
You judge fair, save me / please pay-attention-me
Hurry save me!

Lord himself my rock, my savior / he strong, protect-me
Himself my support, my defender / he lead me for-for his
name honor.

Your face shine-down-on-me, your servant / yourself kind, save me.
Hey, yourselves brave, stand-strong / you trust Lord.

LETTER OF PAUL TO THE ROMANS
(3:21–25, 28)

Brother~sister: Now, law not~need. We look-at-Jesus, see what? God same-as-him holy, right. Law, prophets prove, support. Holy, right, he-give-me how? Believe, faith Jesus Christ. #ALL people same-around, sin; God his glory we earn not-yet. But now we connect-to God, why? because Jesus finish save us. Jesus Christ, God send-him here for suffer, die, our sins forgive. Now we believe possible become holy, right how? Law follow, obey? No, faith only.

Word his Lord.

GOSPEL ACCLAMATION

Alleluia

Myself compare vine (lh), yourself branches (rh)
Suppose you connect-to-me, succeed will you.

HOLY GOSPEL ACCORDING TO MATTHEW (7:21–27)

Disciples, Jesus tell-them, "People name-me Lord, means they touch heaven will? Only #IF my father want they obey. Future day, many people come-to-me (cl:1,1), say, 'Lord, your name we use for predict, devil eliminate, wonderful works succeed.' Finish, I look-at-them, shrug, say, 'I don't-know you. Away.'

Suppose my story you pay-attention, obey, you compare man wise, his house build, rock support. Hit rain, water~flood, wind, house stand-strong. Suppose my story you ignore, forget, don't-care, you compare man stupid, his house build soil <u>sand</u>. Hit rain, water~flood, wind, house collapse, ruin."

Gospel his Lord.

Tenth Sunday in Ordinary Time

BOOK OF THE PROPHET HOSEA
(6:3–6)

During time-period trouble, people say, "Know Lord, we want. We know-that he come will. Sun rise (l), bright, same he come (cl:1) (r), bright, judge. Every-year spring rain all-over, same he come, spread-out."

God says, "My people, I #do-do? Your prayer compare cloud, quick dissolve, continue not. Now I angry, bawl-you-out, how? Prophet, I-inform-him, he-inform-you. Love (r), sacrifice (l), I prefer which? It (love). Know God (r), animal kill, burn (l), important which? It (know God)."

Word his Lord.

RESPONSORIAL PSALM
(50:1, 8, 12–13, 14–15)

Those people good, God power save, I-show-them.

Lord God finish speak, #ALL people inform / all-over earth, east, west, all-over, quote:
"Your sacrifice I accept, myself angry not, / animals you kill, burn, I see, always."

"Suppose I hungry, I tell you? Shhhh / world, everything, #ALL mine! Bull meat I eat, think you? No! / Goat blood I drink? No!"

"Sacrifice-to God you want? Well, praise give-him / your promise++ #DO
Finish, happen time trouble, you summon-me / save-you will I, finish, glory you-give-me will."

LETTER OF PAUL TO THE ROMANS

(4:18–25)

Brother~sister: Long-ago, Abraham believe what? he become father for many people will, why? God promise. He faith wow! Himself old 100, almost ready die; wife <u>Sarah</u> old, baby born not-yet. But God promise, he (Abraham) trust. He faith strong, glory give-to God, believe what? God promise, he expert succeed can. His faith God see, oh-I-see, accept-him. Understand, Abraham, you, same. Your faith God see, oh-I-see, accept. What faith? We believe Jesus, God raise-him-up live again. Jesus die for our sins, no-matter, God raise-him-up live again for save us, become we-connect-God.

Word his Lord.

GOSPEL ACCLAMATION

Alleluia

Lord send-me for-for? People poor, good #NEWS inform; people slave, now free.

HOLY GOSPEL ACCORDING TO MATTHEW

(9:9–13)

Jesus notice man, he name <u>Matthew</u>, sit there <u>tax</u> table. Tell-him, "Come-here." He stand-up, accompany. <u>Matthew</u> house, Jesus go-to for dinner. Sinners many arrive, sit-around-table with Jesus and disciples. Pharisees see, question, "Jesus eat with sinners, why?" Jesus hear, answer, "People healthy, doctor not~need. Sick people, doctor need. Go read Bible, God says, 'Mercy (r), sacrifice (l), I prefer it (mercy).' Myself come for-for? Holy people summon? No, sinners summon."

Gospel his Lord.

Eleventh Sunday in Ordinary Time

BOOK OF EXODUS (19:2–6a)

Desert name <u>Sinai</u>, Israel people arrive, camp set-up. Near mountain, Moses go-up, God meet. Lord tell-him, "Those people Israel, you tell them, quote, 'Egypt people God punish you finish see, but you he protect, bring-you here safe. Now must you pay-attention-him God, his commandments obey; finish, you become his people special, cherish more-than all-over earth. Your kingdom have priest hordes, people holy.' "

Word his Lord.

RESPONSORIAL PSALM (100:1–2, 3, 5)

We his people, he care-for us.

#ALL people, happy sing-to Lord / serve Lord willing, come face-to-face happy sign-ASL.

Know-that Lord himself true God / he make us, cherish us, care-for us.

Lord himself true~work good / himself kind forever, faithful for #ALL people forever.

LETTER OF PAUL TO THE ROMANS (5:6–11)

Brother~sister, Christ finish die for save us sinners. Suppose person true~work good, maybe friend brave willing die in-exchange, possible. But God prove love—how? We sinner no-matter, Christ willing die for save us. Means what? Time God ready punish, Jesus blood protect us. Sin means we, God, enemy; but Jesus die, cause two-of-us connect. Now connect, means saved. We boast what? God, me, connect—how? Jesus, himself cause.

Word his Lord.

GOSPEL ACCLAMATION

Alleluia

God his kingdom near-future happen
Your life change, from-now-on gospel believe.

HOLY GOSPEL ACCORDING TO MATTHEW (9:36—10:8)

People, Jesus see-them, feel~pity, why? They seem lost, abandoned, compare sheep have none shepherd. Jesus tell disciples, "Have people many, but ministers few. Pray for more workers." Apostles twelve, Jesus summon, power give-them. Suppose person devil spirit inside, eliminate; sick, heal. Apostles twelve name: Simon, later name change Peter, brother Andrew; James and brother John, Philip, Bartholomew, Thomas, Matthew [tax collector], James, Thaddeus, Simon and Judas Iscariot, that-one betray him. Jesus tell-them, "Pagan land, Samaritan land, touch not. Go-to Israel people, tell-them God his kingdom near-future happen. Sick, heal; dead, raise, live again; leper, clean; devil, eliminate. Understand, free, pay-you nothing."

Gospel his Lord.

TWELFTH SUNDAY IN ORDINARY TIME

BOOK OF THE PROPHET JEREMIAH

(20:10–13)

<u>Jeremiah</u> said, "Secret gossip I hear. People say, 'Fear (l), dread (r)! Criticize him'—mean me (hon)! Mock-me. They past my friends, now they wait, let's-see I fall, stuck—they jump-at-chance beat-me (shot-h), defeat-me. But Lord himself with-me, support-me. My enemy win not. They fail will, ashamed, confused will. Lord, you test people themselves good; you analyze-mind, analyze-heart. See you punish them, I want—I trust you action right. Sing, praise Lord. Those enemy power, people poor he save~protect."

Word his Lord.

RESPONSORIAL PSALM

(69:8–10, 14, 17, 33–35)

Lord, you love me, please answer-me

For you, I patient~accept insult / myself shame, pull-head-in
My brothers, they reject-me / my family un-popular-me,
Your home, I enthusiastic dwell-on / people, they insult-you,
insult-me same.

Lord, I pray-to you / please, your love send-down
Yourself true kind, please help / answer me, help-me
Lord, please answer-me, you kind excessive / please mercy-me.

You people humble, look, now happy / God you seek, your hearts
now inspire!
People poor, Lord pay-attention / people slave, he forget not
Heaven, earth, whole praise give-to (God) / ocean,
fish praise-him same.

LETTER OF PAUL TO THE ROMANS

Brother~sister, one man cause sin, it sin cause die, means #ALL people die must. Before law, before, world have sin, no-matter law establish not-yet. We think, none law means none sin—wrong. Adam to Moses, #ALL people die, why? Adam sin influence. #BUT God give different. Adam, his sin cause #ALL die, but God fine-wiggle give more! He give Jesus Christ for save #ALL.

Word his Lord.

GOSPEL ACCLAMATION

Alleluia

Lord says, Holy Spirit honest support-me
And future you support-me, proof.

HOLY GOSPEL ACCORDING TO MATTHEW

(10:26–33)

Jesus tell apostles, quote, "Hey, those people, dread-them not. Everything now hide, show will. Everything now secret, inform will. I tell-you private, you announce must. You hear hide, inform must.

Suppose person there kill-you can, but your soul destroy can't—fear him, for-for? Better fear God, body, soul destroy, both, there hell can he. Know-that bird small, buy cheap, trivial, but happen one bird fall-to-ground, die, Father notice. Hair how-many you have, God know. You worth! than bird hordes.

Suppose people you inform-them about me, Father I inform-him about you. Suppose you inform-them refuse, I inform-him refuse."

Gospel his Lord.

THIRTEENTH SUNDAY IN ORDINARY TIME

SECOND BOOK OF KINGS

(4:8–11, 14–16a)

Elisha arrive town name Shunem. Woman, herself important, invite him eat with her. From-then-on, every time Elisha touch town, tend stop, eat there. Woman tell husband, "I know-that he true holy man from God. He visit here from-time-to-time; two-of-us prepare room upstairs, bed, table, chair, light put++—why not? He sleep there can."

Later, servant, Elisha question, "Can I #do-do something for her?" Servant answer, "Yes, she have son none, husband old." (Elisha) "Oh-I-see. Tell her come-here." Woman come (cl:1). (Elisha) "Next year, baby son will you."

Word his Lord.

RESPONSORIAL PSALM

(89:2–3, 16–17, 18–19)

Lord himself good, I announce forever.

Lord, he promise good, I praise forever / people generations, inform-them he faithful will I
His kindness he give forever / there heaven he finish prove himself faithful.

People they happy praise-him, happy they / right way God show-them
Your name they hear, celebrate / you judge fair, promote-them

Yourself give-them strong-wow / you love us, give-us honor
Lord himself protects us / himself holy, our king.

LETTER OF PAUL TO THE ROMANS

(6:3–4, 8–11)

Brother~sister, we baptized, show we connect Christ Jesus, die same-as-him. During baptize, we, quote, "die, bury" with Jesus, same-as-him.

Jesus, Father raise-up live again, same new life he give us will. Suppose we die connect Christ, resurrect connect-him will. We know-that Christ die, resurrect, once finish; again die never. Death defeat-him not. Jesus die for-for? sin destroy; now he lives for God. Same must you sin reject, live for God.

Word his Lord.

GOSPEL ACCLAMATION

Alleluia

Yourselves people special, priest #ALL, holy group
Announce praise-God; dark, he summon-you his wonderful light face-to-face.

HOLY GOSPEL ACCORDING TO MATTHEW (10:37–42)

Jesus tell apostles, quote, "Suppose person love father, mother, son, daughter, more than me, he not worth connect-me. Suppose he suffer refuse, follow me refuse, he not worth connect-me. Suppose life cherish, die will he. But, suppose die for me he willing, live forever will.

Suppose person welcome you, he same welcome me, means he same welcome God—himself sent me. Suppose prophet you welcome because himself prophet, he (prophet) wonderful give-you. Holy man welcome, he (holy man) wonderful give-you. I promise, people humble you water cup-give-them because they follow me, God wonderful give-you will."

Gospel his Lord.

FOURTEENTH SUNDAY IN ORDINARY TIME

BOOK OF THE PROPHET ZECHARIAH (9:9–10)

Celebrate, Zion! Shout happy, Jerusalem! See, your king arrive,
himself savior; humble, donkey ride. Country there name Ephraim,
here Jerusalem, war, he stop, finish. Their bow-and-arrow, he destroy.
He announce peace for #ALL people. He control all-over earth,
from river there to far last place earth.

Word his Lord.

RESPONSORIAL PSALM (145:1–2, 8–9, 10–11, 13–14)

Your name I praise forever, my King, my God.

I praise you, my king, my God / your name I honor forever and ever.
Daily I bless you / your name I praise forever and ever.

Lord true good, mercy / angry postpone, kind excessive.
Lord himself action good for #ALL / he heart-soft, wow.

Lord, whole earth thank-you / your faithful people honor you.
Your kingdom glory we tell-story / your might we announce.

Lord, he promise faithful / his work~action holy
Suppose people fall, he raise-up / suppose oppressed, he help.

LETTER OF PAUL TO THE ROMANS (8:9, 11–13)

Brother~sister, body you cherish not; spirit you cherish, why?
God his spirit connect-to-you. Any person himself have none spirit,
he, God, united not. Happen Jesus die, God raise-him live again.
Suppose God spirit live in you, happen you die, God raise-you live
again same.

We owe, yes, but pay world not. Live follow body thirst not. Die will. Better push-aside, follow spirit thirst—live will.

Word his Lord.

GOSPEL ACCLAMATION

Alleluia

Honor God, Father, Lord control heaven, earth,
Those people humble, heaven secret he show-them.

HOLY GOSPEL ACCORDING TO MATTHEW (11:25–30)

Jesus pray, quote, "Father, yourself Lord control heaven and earth. I praise-you—why? Those people smart, big-brains, you teach-them nothing; but those children, you show-them everything. True~honest, you want that. My Father finish give-me everything. Only Father knows son; only son knows Father; understand, suppose Father I show-you, you know him same-as-me can.

Come, #ALL people tired, burdened; give-you rest will I. My work take-up, copy-me, myself humble, heart gentle. Your soul rest will, why? My work easy, my burden light."

Gospel his Lord.

Fifteenth Sunday in Ordinary Time

BOOK OF THE PROPHET ISAIAH (55:10–11)

Know-that heaven water sprinkle-down soil, wet, cause grow++
finish, water rise-up, dissolve. Grow++ make seed for farmer,
plus grind-up, make bread for people eat. Same compare my word
speak~outward, action++ what I want; finish, #BACK succeed.

Word his Lord.

RESPONSORIAL PSALM (65:10, 11, 12–13, 14)

Good soil, #SEED plant, grow-grow will.

You finish touch soil, water-pour / cause-it grow heap.
God his river full / ready grow.

Soil, you prepare / water sink-in, hard dissolve
Rain cause-it soft / bless, grow.

Year completed, ready harvest / path grow-covered-over, whew!
Area sow-seed not-yet, itself grow / all-over happy.

Field there have sheep / valley there have grow
People sing happy celebrate.

LETTER OF PAUL TO THE ROMANS (8:18–23)

Suffer now, trivial; future glory beat-it (shot-h). True, whole world
eager wait let's-see who true connect God. World itself worthless,
why? World itself decide become worthless?? No, God decide. No-
matter, world have hope, become free, sin dismiss, share glory will
because we children his God. We know-that #ALL people suffer
up-to-now. We have Holy Spirit, yes, but no-matter, we suffer inside
during wait for God save our body.

Word his Lord.

GOSPEL ACCLAMATION

Alleluia

#SEED means word his God, Christ himself farmer
#ALL those follow him, live forever.

HOLY GOSPEL ACCORDING TO MATTHEW (13:1–23)

Jesus out walk, <u>lake</u> near, sit down. Wrong, people flock-to there.
Jesus decide boat sit, people stand-around (cl:4,4). Jesus story, quote,
"One day farmer sow-seed. <u>Seeds</u> throw++ where? Some there path,
birds peck++, all-gone, fly away. Some there hard area, quick grow,
but deep none. Sun shine hot, die. Some <u>seed</u> there grow-twisted-
sharp++; grow, tangled, die. Last, some there good soil, grow++
heap. Warn, every person pay-attention."

Later, disciples question-to him, "You tend teach stories—why?"
Jesus answer, "Secret things about kingdom his God, you understand, but they understand not. Person himself understand, more
understand will. Person he understand little-bit, whole-thing lose.
I teach story—why? They look-at-me, but see not. They listen,
but understand nothing. Long-ago Isaiah wrote about them, quote:
'You listen++, understand none; you look++, see none. Your heart
lazy, ears closed, eyes shut (window). Suppose you see, hear can,
maybe your heart understand. Finish, you follow me, and I heal
you.' But lucky you—why? Your eyes see, your ears hear. Many
saints, prophets wish see, hear, same-as-you, but fail.

Now explain story about farmer. Path, <u>seed</u> there, mean person hear
story about God, but understand zero. Devil easy steal. Hard area
mean person hear story, happy accept, but deep none, quick die.
Happen problem, persecute-me, give-up. There sharp tangled means
person hear story, but other things important, world, money conflict,
tempt, give-up. But there good soil means person hear story, accept
100%. He grow++ succeed."

Gospel his Lord.

Sixteenth Sunday in Ordinary Time

BOOK OF WISDOM

(12:13, 16–19)

Other <u>god</u> compare you have none. You care-for #ALL; you judge right, proof not~need. Your might cause-you think, judge fair; your control cause-you feel mercy. Suppose your power, person skeptical, you show! Prove. Suppose people they know you, but still afraid, you bawl-out. Yourself mighty! No-matter, you judge heart-soft; you control full love, why? Yourself full power. Your action teach what? Suppose people themselves become fair want, kind must they. Your children, you give-them good reason for hope their sin you forgive will.

Word his Lord.

RESPONSORIAL PSALM

(86:5–6, 9–10, 15–16)

Lord, yourself good, forgive-us

Lord, yourself good, please forgive-us / #ALL pray, you kind-to-them
My prayer pay attention / my beg~ASL please notice

#ALL nations you finish make, now they assemble / for worship you, glory give-to your name
Yourself wonderful, your actions perfect / yourself only God

Lord, yourself, full mercy, heart-soft / slow become angry, full kindness and faith
Look-at-me, mercy-me / your strong, give-to-me your servant

LETTER OF PAUL TO THE ROMANS

Ourselves weak, true, but Holy Spirit help-us. How pray, we don't-know, but spirit expert pray for us, use our voice cry-out, but words++ none. Our heart, God know; spirit talk, he understand, why? spirit prays for you way God wants.

Word his Lord.

GOSPEL ACCLAMATION

Alleluia

Honor Father, Lord control heaven and earth
People humble, heaven secret he inform-them.

HOLY GOSPEL ACCORDING TO MATTHEW

Jesus story, quote, "Kingdom his God compare man, field he sow-seed. Night, sleep, enemy come, <u>weeds</u> sow-seed. Later grow; <u>weeds</u> see, puzzled. Servant question-to-him, "You sow-seed good <u>seed</u>, right? Now <u>weeds</u>. How?" (Man) "Enemy." (Servant) "You want us pull++?" (Man) "No-wave; <u>weeds</u> pull++, maybe wrong <u>wheat</u> pull++. Wait, grow, mainstream-up together. Time harvest, I will order divide, <u>weeds</u> tie-up, throw-out, fire; <u>wheat</u> put-in <u>barn</u>."

Other story: "Kingdom his God compare <u>mustard</u> <u>seed</u> person sow-seed. <u>Seed</u> itself tiny, but grow, whew! Big. Birds many fly-there, make home, nest."

Other story: "Kingdom his God compare <u>yeast</u>, woman <u>flour</u> pour-in, knead; later, grow-in-size."

Jesus story these (on fingers) for teach people—why? Long-ago prophet wrote: "I will teach story, things secret world set-up up-to-now, I inform will." Jesus satisfy.

People go-off, disciples ask Jesus story mean what? Jesus said, "Farmer sow-seed, that means Son of Man, me (hon); (2) field means world; (3) good <u>seed</u> means people connect God. (4) <u>Weeds</u> mean people follow devil; (5) enemy that-one <u>weeds</u> sow-seed means devil himself. Harvest means time world end; workers means angels. Remember <u>weeds</u> throw-out, #BURN? Same happen time world end. Son of Man will send angels find people bad, throw-them fire, they cry-out, suffer. People good shine, sun, same. Every person pay-attention must."

Gospel his Lord.

Seventeenth Sunday in Ordinary Time

FIRST BOOK OF KINGS

(3:5, 7–12)

Happen night, King <u>Solomon</u> dream, Lord envision. He (Lord) said,
"Any you ask-for; I give-you." (Solomon) "Lord my God, myself
your servant, but you promote-me king follow my father <u>David</u>.
I young me; I don't-know #do-do. I serve you here your special
people, many, hordes, count altogether how-many can't (^). Please
give-me heart full understanding—for-for? Judge your people can
I, know right, wrong. Who can control your people hordes?"

Lord listen, his prayer give-him. God said, "You pray for long life?
No. Rich? No. Your enemy I kill? No. You pray for heart wise;
know right, wrong you want. I accept. Heart whew! wise, understand
I-give-you. Other person equal-you up-to-now, from-now-on, none."

Word his Lord.

RESPONSORIAL PSALM

(19:57, 72, 76–77, 127–128, 129–130)

Lord, your commandment I love.

Lord, I know-that / my duty what? your word obey
Law you speak, itself precious / more-than gold, silver heap.

Yourself kind, mercy-me / same you promise your servant
Please, mercy-me, live~continue will I / your law I cherish.

Your commandment I love / more-than gold fine
Your law lead-me right way / wrong way I hate.

Your rules true wonderful / I follow willing
Your word give-me light / people humble understand can.

LETTER OF PAUL TO THE ROMANS

(8:28–30)

We know-that everything work harmony for people themselves love God. He summon them; he know them, want Jesus share—why? Want Jesus have brother~sister many. First, he know; (2), he summon; (3), he forgive, connect; (4), glory he give-them.

Word his Lord.

GOSPEL ACCLAMATION

Alleluia

Honor Father, control heaven, earth;
people humble, heaven secret he teach-them.

HOLY GOSPEL ACCORDING TO MATTHEW

(13:44–52)

Jesus inform people hordes: "Kingdom his God compare field have money bury there, man find. (look around) Money hide, excited; go: everything he have, sell; money, field buy. Other example: Kingdom heaven compare man, himself seller; search perfect <u>pearl</u>. Find, everything he have, sell; <u>pearl</u> buy.

Kingdom his God also compare <u>net</u>, water-area throw-into, pull out, many things stuck there++. Open, sit down, look-it-over; good things, put-in-container++; worthless there++, throw-out. That compare world end. Future, angels separate people good, people bad. This (bad) group, throw-out fire, cry-out, suffer. Understand you?"

Apostles "#YES." (Jesus) "Every <u>scribe</u> himself big-brains Kingdom God, he compare man have house. It house have many things, old, new both."

Gospel his Lord.

EIGHTEENTH SUNDAY IN ORDINARY TIME

BOOK OF THE PROPHET ISAIAH

(55:1–3)

Thirsty you-all? Come-here, water. Money none? Come-here, food have. Come, pay none, cost none. Wine, milk drink. Money spend for things can't eat, why? Satisfy not. Pay-attention-me, eat good, enjoy. Come-here me (hon), pay-attention-me, live will you. I again promise united-with-you, same long-ago I promise connect <u>David</u>.

Word his Lord.

RESPONSORIAL PSALM

(145:8–9, 15–16, 17–18)

Lord himself feeds-us. Our needs he notice.

Lord himself heart-soft, mercy-us / angry postpone, kindness excessive
Lord care-for #ALL / he make++, cherish

#ALL people look-to you full hope/ time-right you give-them satisfy
Everything you give-give-give / we quick satisfy.

Lord-his actions true fair / his work holy.
#ALL summon Lord, he pay-attention, / understand, they pray full honest.

LETTER OF PAUL TO THE ROMANS

(8:35, 37–39)

Christ, his love, cut (scissors), separate (from me), how? Struggle cause two-of-us disconnect? Worry? Persecution? Hunger? Naked? Danger? Die? Happen these-things (on fingers), no-matter; we succeed because he loves us. I believe true, have nothing—(1) life, death; (2) angel, devil; (3) now time, future time; (4) high place, deep place; (5) other people—nothing can cut God, his love separate. His love we know how? through Jesus Christ our Lord.

Word his Lord.

GOSPEL ACCLAMATION

Alleluia

Bread only satisfy not,
God speak, every word we depend-on for live.

HOLY GOSPEL ACCORDING TO MATTHEW (14:13–21)

Happen Jesus hear little-story John Baptist die, go (cl:1) boat, sit-in, alone. People hear, decide flock-there, meet-him. Jesus look-around crowd, feel-pity; there++ sick, influence heal. Sunset, disciples said, "Here empty. Tell people go town, food buy for themselves." Jesus said, "Go town, not~need. Self food give-them." (Disciples) "We have nothing. Well, bread five, fish two have." (Jesus) "Bring-here." Heaven Jesus look-up, pray bless, break, give-them disciples; they share++. #ALL people eat, satisfied. Food left, twelve baskets full. People eat altogether how-many? Men, about 5,000, plus women and children.

Gospel his Lord.

NINETEENTH SUNDAY IN ORDINARY TIME

FIRST BOOK OF KINGS

(19:9, 11–13)

Mountain name <u>Horeb</u>, <u>Elijah</u> arrive, <u>cave</u> find, enter. Lord said, "Come-out, stand, wait; Lord pass-by will." Happen strong wind, blow, rocks roll-down, destroy—but Lord not there. Second, earth-quake—but Lord not there. Third fire—but Lord not there. Last, quiet hear. Happen Elijah hear, know that-one Lord, (mime) face hide in coat, <u>cave</u> walk-to (cl:1).

Word his Lord.

RESPONSORIAL PSALM

(85:9, 10, 11–12, 13–14)

Lord, your kindness please show-us, save us.

God announce, I pay-attention / Lord announce peace
People honor him, save-them will he / glory touch our country.

Kindness (l), honest (r), unite / judge~fair (l), peace (r), harmonize
Earth, grow, it <u>truth</u> / there heaven judge~fair have.

Lord himself bless earth / our land grow increase++
God himself judge fair / prepare for himself arrive.

LETTER OF PAUL TO THE ROMANS

(9:1–5)

I speak honest; lie none me. Holy Spirit knows I grieve true. I willing myself, Christ, disconnect, #IF possible save you Israel people. God finish adopt you, his glory, his promise, his law share; worship, he teach-you; ancestors he give-you, generations-forward, born Messiah [understand, I mean his human generations]. Bless God, himself control everything.

Word his Lord.

GOSPEL ACCLAMATION

Alleluia

I wait-for Lord,
his little-story my soul wait-for.

HOLY GOSPEL ACCORDING TO MATTHEW   (14:22–33)

People eat, satisfied; finish, Jesus tell disciples get-in boat-to-there.
Jesus himself (cl:1) go mountain, pray alone, time sunset. Night,
disciples storm, boat toss. Time three morning. Water, Jesus walk
(cl:V-legs on back of hand). Disciples notice, scared! "Ghost there!"
scared, scream++. Jesus said, "Calm down. That me (hon). Afraid
finish!" Peter said, "Lord, #IF true~work you, tell-me walk meet-
you." (Jesus) "Come." Peter boat get-out, water walk (cl:V-legs on
hand), toward meet. Wrong, feel wind strong, look-around (cl:f,f),
scared, sink, cry-out, "Lord, help-me!" Quick Jesus grab-him. "Faith
little-bit you! Afraid, why?" Two-of-them get-in boat, wind reduce,
dissolve. Other disciples boat look-at-him, honor, said, "True, you
Son his God."

Gospel his Lord.

TWENTIETH SUNDAY IN ORDINARY TIME

BOOK OF THE PROPHET ISAIAH

(56:1, 6–7)

Lord says, "Action right, save-you will I. Judge-you near-future, I. People themselves unite-to Lord, (2) honor Lord, (3) love my name, (4) serve me, (5) keep seventh day holy and obey my law, those people I bring heaven, give-them happy. Their sacrifice, I accept. My church become name, quote, 'house for pray' for #ALL people."

Word his Lord.

RESPONSORIAL PSALM

(67:2–3, 5, 6, 8)

God, #ALL people praise-you.

God, please mercy-us, bless-us / please look-at-me, shine-on-me
Here earth, your way we can know / #ALL people know you save-us.

#ALL people happy, celebrate / why? You control people fair
#ALL countries, you lead.

We praise-you, God / #ALL people praise you
Please bless us / finish, people all-over earth honor-you.

LETTER OF PAUL TO THE ROMANS

(11:13–15, 29–32)

You non-Jew people, inform-you: I happy preach-to-you, why? Hope those Jew people see, jealous; maybe connect, save. First, Jesus, Jew people reject, kill—succeed sin forgive. Now, suppose they change, Jesus accept, means what? Past dead, now rise live again! God give, later take-away never. God summon, later mind-change never. You yourselves past disobey God, now he mercy-you. Jew people now disobey, but God mercy-them will. #ALL people God allow disobey, why? Mercy show.

Word his Lord.

GOSPEL ACCLAMATION

Alleluia

Jesus story~gospel, God his kingdom announce;
People sick++, Jesus heal.

HOLY GOSPEL ACCORDING TO MATTHEW (15:21–28)

Jesus travel area <u>Tyre</u> and <u>Sidon</u>. Woman, herself non-Jew, she come (cl:1), said, "Lord, mercy-me. My daughter have devil inside, awful." Jesus answer nothing. Apostles complain woman bother-me, go-away. Jesus tell-them, "My goal care-for Israel people only." Woman bow, honor, said, "Lord, help-me." But Jesus said, "What! Family food take, give-to dogs?" (Woman) "You name-me dog, but suppose family food table fall-off, dog eat." Jesus look-at-her, "Faith, wow!" Give-her, instant daughter heal.

Gospel his Lord.

Twenty-First Sunday in Ordinary Time

BOOK OF THE PROPHET ISAIAH

Man name <u>Shebna</u>, himself boss-most, God tell-him, quote, "You sit, control; throw-you-out will I. You power most, I demote-to-baby-finger will. Same day, my servant name <u>Eliakim</u> I summon, himself son <u>Hilkiah</u> his. Your clothes, I give-him; your belt, I give-him; your authority, I give-him. He will become quote 'father' for people live there Jerusalem all-over. I give-him responsible for family <u>David</u> descendants. Suppose he open, who shut, who? None. Suppose he shut, who open? None. Establish him stand-strong will I; his family honor-him will."

Word his Lord.

RESPONSORIAL PSALM

(138:1–2, 2–3, 6, 8)

Lord, your love continue forever. You finish make us; abandon us not.

I thank-you Lord from my heart / why? My prayer you pay-attention
With angels I sing praise you / there your holy place I worship.

I thank you / because yourself kind, honest
Happen I cry out, you answer / strong, you give-me excess.

Lord himself high, but people humble he notice / people proud he knows
Lord, your kindness continue forever / abandon us not.

LETTER OF PAUL TO THE ROMANS

Lord, his knowledge, his wisdom true complex, whew. His judge, we analyze impossible. His tend, we understand impossible. Who knows Lord his thoughts? Who advise-him? Suppose person give-him first, Lord pay-him #BACK must? #ALL things come from him, and through him, and for him. Glory give-him forever. Amen (in palm)!

Word his Lord.

GOSPEL ACCLAMATION

Alleluia

Yourself Peter, now I name-you Rock;
that rock my church I establish,
Devil destroy never.

HOLY GOSPEL ACCORDING TO MATTHEW

Area <u>Caesarea</u> <u>Philippi</u> Jesus arrive, ask disciples, "People they gossip about me (hon)—say what?" (Disciples) "Few say you <u>John</u> Baptist, other say you <u>Elijah</u>, other few say you <u>Jeremiah</u> or other prophet." (Jesus) "Oh-I-see. You say what?" <u>Simon</u> <u>Peter</u> said, "Yourself Messiah, son his God." (Jesus) "Wow! Bless you, <u>Simon</u>. Who inform-you about me? People? (shake head no) My Father heaven inform-you. Now I name-you <u>Rock</u>; that rock my church I establish. Devil destroy never. I give-you what? Quote 'key,' heaven open can you. How? Suppose you decide bound here earth, I order bound there heaven. Suppose you decide free here earth, I order free there heaven same-as-here." Finish, Jesus tell disciples, "Inform-all myself Messiah, no-wave. Confidential."

Gospel his Lord.

Twenty-Second Sunday in Ordinary Time

BOOK OF THE PROPHET JEREMIAH (20:7–9)

Lord, you deceive-me, and I gullible, accept. You strong, beat-me (shot-h). All-day, people mock-me. Every time I speak, I cry-out angry, destroy. Word his Lord cause-me shame, mock-me all-day. I decide, "I talk about him nothing! Say his name, refuse me." But, wrong, my heart fire-rise, restrain bore me. Endure-it can't me; express must.

Word his Lord.

RESPONSORIAL PSALM (63:2, 3–4, 5–6, 8–9)

My soul thirst-for you, Lord my God.

God, myself search-for you; / my body, my soul thirst for you.
Compare earth dry / thirst-for water.

There heaven I look-at you / your power, glory, I want see
Your kindness (r), life (l), it (kindness) better; / your glory I sign-ASL.

During life I honor you; / I sign-ASL, your name summon.
My soul satisfy compare banquet~heap / myself happy give-you praise.

Yourself my helper / connect-you I sing happy.
My soul cherish you / your strong hand support-me.

LETTER OF PAUL TO THE ROMANS (12:1–2)

Brother~sister, I beg, your body give-to God same compare holy, living sacrifice; God accept, why? Show true worship. Yourself follow, harmonize world? No. Your life change, God give-you mind new, his want you know can; action good, perfect, can.

Word his Lord.

GOSPEL ACCLAMATION

Alleluia

Lord Jesus Christ, his Father please help-you understand
Oh-I-see, wonderful hope he offer-you.

HOLY GOSPEL ACCORDING TO MATTHEW   (16:21–27)

Jesus story Jerusalem he must go-to, suffer, die, bury, third day resurrect. Peter tap-(Jesus)-on-shoulder, beckon, two-of-them walk-together (cl:1,1), private discuss. (Peter) "Awful happen++, God protect will." Jesus bawl-him-out! "You devil, away! You try cause-me sin. God think, you understand not. Only people think, you understand."

Finish, Jesus inform apostles: Suppose person, follow me he want, forget himself must he, patient suffer accept, follow me. Person want life safe, die will he; but person willing life give-up for me, live will. Suppose man succeed whole world win, but lose himself—worthless. He pay exchange for save soul, what? He have nothing. Son of Man (hon) will come full Father glory with angels popular (cl:1,5)—for-for? Pay each person depend his++ actions.

Gospel his Lord.

TWENTY-THIRD SUNDAY IN ORDINARY TIME

BOOK OF THE PROPHET EZEKIEL

(33:7–9)

God says, quote, "I appoint you 'supervisor' for Israel people. I talk, you listen, inform-them, warn, must you. Suppose sinner I tell-him he will die; you go warn, help, teach refuse, he die will, but blame-you for his die. Understand, suppose you go warn, help, teach; he change, improve refuse, he die will, but you live continue."

Word his Lord.

RESPONSORIAL PSALM

(95:1–2, 6–7, 8–9)

Suppose today you feel God summon-me, resist not.

Come, happy sing (to) Lord / praise our savior
Face-to-face, thank-him / happy sing sign-ASL-to-him.

Come, bow-down, worship / kneel face-to-face Lord, himself made us
Himself our God / he cherish, care-for us.

Suppose today God summon-you you feel / resist not
Same long-ago your ancestors resist / my work they see, trust not.

LETTER OF PAUL TO THE ROMANS

(13:8–10)

We owe money none, but we owe God what? Love each-other must. Reason? Law, love satisfy. Commandments (1) adultery not, (2) kill not, (3) steal not, (4) drool~want++ not, list-down, one sentence #ALL (down fingers) include: You love yourself, love other people same. Other people love, hurt-them never, so . . . law, love satisfies.

Word his Lord.

GOSPEL ACCLAMATION

Alleluia

Christ cause God, people connect, inform-all forgive succeed.

HOLY GOSPEL ACCORDING TO MATTHEW (18:15–20)

Jesus tell apostles, "Suppose your brother action wrong against you—#do-do? Go, private tell-him you angry reason. Suppose he listen, accept, succeed friends again. But, suppose he stubborn argue, summon two~three people come (cl:3); two-of-us quarrel, three-of-them listen, prove. Suppose three-of-them he ignore, go face-to-face church. Suppose church he ignore, reject him same not-Jew <u>or</u> tax collector. I promise, suppose you decide bound here earth, I order bound heaven. Suppose you decide free here, I order free heaven same-as-here. Again I tell-you: suppose two people pray together for something, my Father give will. Happen people two, three assemble my name, I connect."

Gospel his Lord.

TWENTY-FOURTH SUNDAY IN ORDINARY TIME

BOOK OF SIRACH

(27:30—28:7)

Anger (index finger), hate (middle finger), two-of-them awful, but sinner cherish them (on two fingers). People they tend get-even++, Lord get-even-them will, why? Their sins many (on fingers) he remember. Better what? Other people wrong, forgive; finish, happen you pray, your sin, Lord forgive. Suppose man irritated, dwell-on-grudge other person, he expect God forgive him, can he? Suppose man forgive refuse, he pray his sin God forgive, can he? Suppose he dwell-on-grudge, forgive refuse, who forgive him, who? Remember, future you die. Quarrel push-aside, sin stop. Remember commandments, other people hate not. Remember God his promise~connect; those (people) wrong++, ignore.

Word his Lord.

RESPONSORIAL PSALM

(103:1–2, 3–4, 9–10, 11–12)

Lord himself kind, mercy-out, angry not-yet, love excessive.

My soul honor Lord / his holy name I praise
My soul honor Lord / his benefit I remember (on fingers).

Your sin, he forgive / your sick, he heal
Your life ruin, he save / kind, love, he give-you.

He bawl-you-out not / his angry continue forever, no
Our sin he punish not / our wrong punish equal, not he.

Earth, heaven high far / same-as people love him, his love excessive
East, west opposite far / same-as our sin God take-from-left, throw-right.

LETTER OF PAUL TO THE ROMANS

(14:7–9)

No person lives for himself alone, and no person dies for himself alone. During life, we serve Lord; time die, we serve-him still. Christ die finish, rise live again, reason? Become Lord over people dead, living, both, he want.

Word his Lord.

GOSPEL ACCLAMATION

Alleluia

Lord says, quote, "New commandment I give-you,
I love you, same-same you love each-other."

HOLY GOSPEL ACCORDING TO MATTHEW

(8:21–35)

Peter question-to Jesus, "Lord, suppose my brother hurt me, I forgive him how-many times must I? Seven?" (Jesus) "No, not seven times. I tell-you, forgive seventy multiply seven times. Kingdom his God compare king, he decide count, figure how-much people there++ owe. First man meet, he owe money whew! Pay can't. King order must sell man himself, plus wife, children, land, house, everything sell, money receive. Man beg, 'Please, patience, I pay #BACK whole-thing.' King pity, debt (owe) forgive. Later, same man meet other servant, he (other) owe him money little-bit. He grab, shake, said, 'You owe-me, pay-me now!' Servant beg, 'Give-me time, pay-you will I.' Man refuse, throw-him prison. Other servants few see happen, upset, go-to king, inform-him recent happen. King summon man, said, 'Worthless you. You beg, I debt cancel. Why not you mercy other servant, why?' Finish, king hand-him jail, beat-him, stay until he pay-off full. Same my Father punish you, understand, brother, sister you forgive refuse."

Gospel his Lord.

Twenty-Fifth Sunday in Ordinary Time

BOOK OF THE PROPHET ISAIAH

(55:6–9)

Search-for Lord now, why? Possible find him. Cry-out-to-him now, why? He near. Sinner, your life change now. Sin thought, push-aside. Look-at Lord, ask mercy-me; God always forgive. Lord says, "My thought, your thought, same not. My way, your way, different. Know-that heaven high, earth far! separate? That compare my way, your way separate; my thought, your thought separate."

Word his Lord.

RESPONSORIAL PSALM

(145:2–3, 8–9, 17–18)

Suppose Lord you summon, he come (cl:1).

Every-day I honor you / your name I praise forever
Lord himself wonderful, we praise-him/ his power understand, impossible.

Lord himself kind, mercy / angry postpone, love excessive
For #ALL people Lord action good / everything he make++, cherish.

Everything Lord judge fair / everything he make holy
Suppose you summon-him, he come / understand, you summon-him honest.

LETTER OF PAUL TO THE PHILIPPIANS

(1:20–24)

Christ, he receive glory, how? I give-him, no-matter I live, die, no-matter. For me, quote, "<u>life</u>" means Christ; so, die (r) means profit. But, suppose continue live here earth (l), means work, succeed. Prefer which (point, point), don't-know. I feel fascinated-up-right, fascinated-down-left. I want die (r), go live with Christ, because it better than it

(l) (earth); #BUT important I continue live, help-you, teach-you. On-the-fence. Hey! Live right, honor gospel his Christ.

Word his Lord.

GOSPEL ACCLAMATION

Alleluia

Lord, help-us heart-open,
your son his teaching accept.

HOLY GOSPEL ACCORDING TO MATTHEW (20:1–16)

Jesus story: God, his kingdom compare man rich, time sunrise he go, workers hire++ for grapes harvest. Discuss, agree pay how-much, they go-there work. Later, time midmorning, man notice them men idle, hire go-there work, promise pay fair. Again time noon, time mid-afternoon, same happen. Last, late-afternoon man go, notice them men stand++. "Why you idle all-day, why?" "None hire-me." "Go, work."

Night, man tell manager, "Workers, come-here, pay; understand, last group pay first, pass-turn-to-first-group, pay-them last." Workers line-up, last group, pay-them how-much? Full all-day pay. Pass-turn pay++, there first group think, whew, pay-me excessive, will he. Enthusiastic. Wrong, pay same. They complain, "Those men work short, one-hour, trivial. We work all-day, work++ sweat. But you pay-them same-as-us. Not-fair!"

Man said, "My friend, I fair. Two-of-us agree pay-you how-much, right? Well? Have money, go home. That man hire last, I decide pay-him same-as-you. My money, I can think-myself. I give-him same-as-you, you jealous, you?"

See? First, demote-to-baby-finger and last promote-to-thumb will.

Gospel his Lord.

TWENTY-SIXTH SUNDAY IN ORDINARY TIME

BOOK OF THE PROPHET EZEKIEL
(18:25–28)

You say, "Lord, his way not-fair!" Hey, pay-attention. ?? My way not-fair? Maybe your way not-fair. Suppose good man decide good, right, push-aside, go-ahead sin, he die—why? Because he sin. But suppose bad man decide sin push-aside; action good, right, he save life. Up-to-now sin++, now push-aside, he live, die not.

Word his Lord.

RESPONSORIAL PSALM
(25:4–5, 6–7, 8–9)

Lord, please remember mercy-us.

Lord, your way, show-me / your want teach-me
Lead me, teach me honest / yourself my God, my savior.

Please remember mercy-me, Lord / you love me up-to-now
Long-ago young, I sin / myself weak, please you dwell-on not
Yourself kind, remember me / yourself heart-soft, Lord.

Lord himself good, right / sinners, he show-them right way
Humble, he lead-them right, / his way he teach-them.

LETTER OF PAUL TO THE PHILIPPIANS
(2:1–11)

You encourage each-other should, love, comfort, mercy each-other should. I ask-you, give-me happy, how? Think same-around, love same-around, goal same-around. Compete, boast, no-wave; better each person humble, think other important than me, willing help++. They help-me, not~need. Attitude same Christ must you; himself God true, but he willing humble born slave, born man. He obey, accept die cross, wow! Finish, God raise Jesus live again, give-him name exceed. Now, happen Jesus name hear, every person must kneel, no-matter where: heaven, earth, under earth, no-matter, and every voice announce, give glory God Father, quote, "Jesus Christ true Lord!"

Word his Lord.

GOSPEL ACCLAMATION

Alleluia

Lord says, My voice, my sheep hear.
I know them; they follow-me.

HOLY GOSPEL ACCORDING TO MATTHEW   (21:28–32)

Priest, people hordes, Jesus say, "Think-think you? Man have son two. Older son, father meet, said, 'Go work there grape-grow-area.' (Son) 'OK' but go never. Second son man meet, say same-as-first. (Son) 'Refuse, me.' Later sorry, go work. Son obey father, which?" (People) "Second son." (Jesus) "I inform-you, sinners touch heaven before you. Happen past John preach way holy, you believe not, but sinners believe, follow. You finish see-them, still believe refuse."

Gospel his Lord.

Twenty-Seventh Sunday in Ordinary Time

BOOK OF THE PROPHET ISAIAH
(5:1–7)

I story now about my friend, his grape-grow-area. Friend work, dig, rocks eliminate++, grapes plant++. <u>Tower</u> (cl:c,c) build, sit, watch; also make wine machine. Finish, wait grapes grow—wrong! <u>Wild</u> grapes.

Now I ask you-all judge me and my grape-area. My grapes, I #do-do more, what? I work++, care-for++, why grow <u>wild</u> grapes, why? My plan I inform-you. Grape grow-area, #do-do me? Ruin! Fence tear-down; cow, sheep march, graze, don't-care. Clouds, I command rain, shhh.

Grape-area compare what? Israel people. Grapes themselves compare people its <u>Judah</u>. God look, expect things good, right see; wrong, blood he see. He expect fair see; wrong, people cry-out, suffer he hear.

Word his Lord.

RESPONSORIAL PSALM
(80:9, 12, 13–14, 15–16, 19–20)

Israel itself compare God his grape-area

We compare grape~plant there Egypt / God move-here protect, care-for
Plant; it succeed, grow / spread-out all-over

But now you abandon-us why? / Our grapes, enemy steal
#WILD animal walk-on-it squish / cow graze-on-it, all-gone.

Please, Lord, again / heaven look-down, see
Your plant care-for / yourself finish plant-it, now protect
Itself (plant) compare your people / you give-them strong.

Finish, we cherish-you will / new life give-us, your name we depend
Lord God help-us / look-down-on us, save-us please.

LETTER OF PAUL TO THE PHILIPPIANS

Worry, push-aside. Pray, thanks, tell God you need these-things (on fingers). Finish, God his peace whew! your heart, mind touch through Jesus Christ. Last, think focus things true, honest, pure, right, holy, good, worth praise. My preach you finish hear, my action you finish see, now you follow. Finish, God with-you, peace he-give-you.

Word his Lord.

GOSPEL ACCLAMATION

Alleluia

Lord says, I choose you:
all-over world, go, preach succeed.

HOLY GOSPEL ACCORDING TO MATTHEW

Priest and leader, Jesus tell-story: "Grape-grow-area man plant, fence, tower-sit-on-top. Finish, farmers he hire work there. Man himself travel. Time harvest, man send servants go, grapes divide, bring (half). Servants come (cl:3), farmers see, grab, kill. Second time, man send servants many, go-in-group, but same happen again, kill. Last, his son man send, think, 'My son they respect will.' But, son farmers see, say, 'Happen father die, everything take-up will he. Kill-him, why-not? Later, father die, we take-up everything.' Agree++ son (cl:1) grab-him, kill. Future man arrive home, #do-do think you?" (People) "Those bad farmers kill will he; finish, other farmers find, themselves honest, pay-him grapes half." Jesus said, "Finish you read Bible verse, 'Stone, it, builders reject; now it most important stone. Lord himself cause happen. We think wonderful.' I inform-you, God his kingdom he will take-from-you, give-to other people, they action right."

Gospel his Lord.

TWENTY-EIGHTH SUNDAY IN ORDINARY TIME

BOOK OF THE PROPHET ISAIAH

(25:6–10)

Here mountain, #ALL people Lord give-them, what? Food wonderful, wine delicious, feast. Here mountain, #ALL people, #ALL countries have dark influence-them; that dark, Lord destroy: die, it, he destroy-it forever. Cry? Lord God wipe-away-tears will. Feel shame? God remove. Lord himself finish speak. Same day, people will say, "See our God. We up-to-now wait he save-us. There Lord we trust. Now we celebrate, happy, why? He finish save us." Lord, his hand touch this mountain will.

Word his Lord.

RESPONSORIAL PSALM

(23:1–3a, 3b–4, 5, 6)

Lord his house I live there forever and ever

Lord he my care-er; everything I need, he give-me.
There grass~area, he give-me rest;
Near river quiet he lead me / my soul he inspire.

Right way he lead-me for his name honor.
Suppose dark valley I walk (cl:1) no-matter, I fear none;
He here with-me, accompany, full power, might / courage give-me.

Banquet he prepare, / my enemies look-at-me
my head he anoint; / my cup (lh) fill-up-overflow.

God, his good, kind touch my life
Die, I live there his home for ever and ever.

LETTER OF PAUL TO THE PHILIPPIANS

(4:12–14, 19–20)

I finish experience poor, rich, both. I finish learn live happy, no-matter food plenty, hungry; no-matter money comfortable, money blow-off-hand. No-matter—why? Christ give-me strong for succeed. You kind, help-me during my difficult struggle. Everything you need, God give-you, because he rich. What rich? Christ Jesus, he-give-you. Whole glory sign-ASL God Father forever and ever. Amen (in palm)!

Word his Lord.

GOSPEL ACCLAMATION

Alleluia

Lord Jesus Christ, his Father please help-you understand Oh-I-see, wonderful hope he offer-you.

HOLY GOSPEL ACCORDING TO MATTHEW (22:1–14)

Priest, leaders hordes, Jesus again story: "Kingdom his God compare king, he plan wedding party for son. Servants he send go invite++ people come, but they (people) refuse. More servants man send, 'Hey, tell-them food cook finish, everything ready. Come, feast.' People, they ignore, one go-to farm, other go-to business. Other grab servant, beat, kill. King furious, send army go kill those people, their city burn-down. Finish, king tell servants, 'Feast ready, but people I invite not worth. Now you go, road, meet++, invite++ #ALL.' Servants obey, invite++ good, bad, no-matter, bring. Wedding room full hordes. Happen king enter, notice man, he dress not~right for wedding. King say, 'My friend, you come here dressed not~right, why?' Man gulp. King tell servants, 'Hands, feet tie-up, throw-out dark, suffer, cry-out.' God invite many, but accept few."

Gospel his Lord.

TWENTY-NINTH SUNDAY IN ORDINARY TIME

BOOK OF THE PROPHET ISAIAH (45:1, 4–6)

King name <u>Cyrus</u>, Lord choose; support-him; cause other countries humble bow face-to-face him; kings there++ hurry serve him; doors there++ open for him enter; gates barrier? No, bar-up, enter (cl:1). <u>Cyrus</u>, Lord tell-him, "For benefit Israel, your name I summon. You don't-know me, no-matter, name honor I give-you. Myself Lord, other <u>god</u> equal have none. You don't-know me, no-matter, I protect you, why? #ALL people spread-out look-at-you (cl:4,4), know I Lord, other have none."

Word his Lord.

RESPONSORIAL PSALM (96:1, 3, 4–5, 7–8, 9–10)

Glory, honor, give-to Lord.

New song sign-ASL-to Lord / #ALL people sing-to Lord
His glory announce-to #ALL countries / his wonderful actions inform-them.

Lord himself wonderful, praise him / he powerful more-than other <u>gods</u>
Those countries, their <u>gods</u> trivial / but our God, sky he finish make.

You people #ALL countries, / glory, praise give-to Lord.
His name, glory / bring face-to-face-him, give-him.

Clothes holy put-on, worship Lord / #ALL people face-to-face-him, dread
#ALL countries, inform-them Lord true king / #ALL people he control fair.

FIRST LETTER OF PAUL TO THE THESSALONIANS (1:1–5)

<u>Paul</u>, <u>Silvanus</u>, <u>Timothy</u>, three-of-us write, send-to church theirs <u>Thessalonians</u>. You connect God Father and Lord Jesus Christ. Grace, peace touch you. We thank++ God for #ALL you, and we pray for you, inform God your faith you prove, work full love, and continue believe, trust Lord Jesus Christ. We know God love you, choose you, how? Gospel, we preach; you listen (hmm) ?—no; you enthuse, inspire; Holy Spirit influence.

Word his Lord.

GOSPEL ACCLAMATION

Alleluia

God his word cherish,
finish, you shine-bright compare light-bulb shine.

HOLY GOSPEL ACCORDING TO MATTHEW (22:15–21)

<u>Pharisees</u> meet, discuss, plan how Jesus "knock." Few-of-them group-go, tell Jesus, "Teacher, we know-that you true honest man, you teach God his way. You butter-up, nothing. Your opinion, tell-us. Rome king, Jews pay-him tax must?" Their plan Jesus know, said, "You hypocrites! You try trick-me, why? Coin for pay tax, give-me." (hand over coin) "Picture there, who? Name who?" (respond) "<u>Caesar</u>." (Jesus) "Well, <u>Caesar</u> give-him his, but God give-him his."

Gospel his Lord.

THIRTIETH SUNDAY IN ORDINARY TIME

BOOK OF EXODUS   (22:20–26)

Person from other country, oppress-him not—why? Yourselves long-ago live there Egypt. Suppose have <u>widow</u>, (2) <u>orphan</u>, you hurt two-of-them, they cry-out, I pay-attention-them will; angry, sword kill you, cause your wife become <u>widow</u>, your children become <u>orphan</u>. Suppose those people poor, money you loan-them, require-them interest pay-me? No. Suppose coat he give-you, show promise pay, you give #BACK before sunset must—why? Coat he need for warm, sleep. #IF he cry-out, complain, I hear, pity-him.

Word his Lord.

RESPONSORIAL PSALM   (18:2–3, 3–4, 47, 51)

I love you, Lord. You give-me strong

I love you, Lord. You give me strong /
Lord, you support-me, protect, save me.

My God, you give-me place safe / yourself my protector, my savior
I announce, "Praise Lord" / my enemy, you save-me.

Lord, he true~work live, I honor-him / praise God, my Savior
Myself king, you give-me succeed / your love, kindness you give-me.

FIRST LETTER OF PAUL TO THE THESSALONIANS   (1:5–10)

Past, we work socialize-with you, you see we action, help++, work++. Now your-turn copy-us, copy Lord. His word, you accept. You suffer, no-matter, still happy, why? Holy Spirit inspire. You now become example for other believers they live countries different++. Word his Lord spread, begin here, spread all-over; there++ your faith God people see, celebrate. Means what? We preach++, not~need. People there++ already know story about you. What story? You listen-to us, <u>idol</u> (statue) throw-out, God accept; serve him want. You now wait-for his Son heaven come-down (cl:1)—that-one die, resurrect finish—Jesus. Happen time future God angry, ready punish, Jesus save us.

Word his Lord.

GOSPEL ACCLAMATION

Alleluia

Lord says, Any person love me, my command he obey,
my Father love him, two-of-us touch, inspire him.

HOLY GOSPEL ACCORDING TO MATTHEW   (10:46–52)

Pharisees, they hear story Jesus "between-the-eyes" (to other group), they meet, discuss, question-to Jesus, "You know commandments ten? Most important, which?" Jesus answer, (1) "Love God full heart, full soul, full mind must you. It most important commandment. (2) Almost same-as-first: You love yourself, other people love same. These-two commandments, whole law long-list and prophet preach summarize these-two."

Gospel his Lord.

THIRTY-FIRST SUNDAY IN ORDINARY TIME

BOOK OF THE PROPHET MALACHI

(1:14—2:2, 8–10)

Lord say, "Myself wonderful king. My name, people #ALL countries honor. You priests, I command you. Suppose you pay-attention-me refuse, suppose honor glory give-me you enthused not, punish you will I. Past, I bless-you, now destroy-you. Why? You backslide, teach++ wrong, many people you cause-them sin. My agree~connect Israel, you ruin. Now I cause you embarrass, shame face-to-face those people, why? My way you follow not. Happen you judge, you tend favor, support one person than other. We #ALL have one Father, right? One God made #ALL. Why we not fair-around each-other, why? Long-ago agree~connect, you disconnect, why?"

Word his Lord.

RESPONSORIAL PSALM

(131:1, 2, 3)

Lord, I connect-you, peace have.

Lord, my heart humble, / myself snobbish not.
I work, goal arrogant not, / willing humble me.

Now, myself calm, quiet / my soul feel~same child.
You care-for me compare same mother care-for baby / Now my soul calm, satisfy.

You people Israel trust Lord, / now and forever.

FIRST LETTER OF PAUL TO THE THESSALONIANS

(2:7–9, 13)

During we live there with you, we heart-soft compare mother cherish baby. We love you so-much, we want share what? God his good #NEWS, same our life we want share. You remember we work all-day, all-night, money earn, same-time preach God his inform—why?

155

Take-advantage, mooch, don't-want. Now we thank++ God because his inform you accept. You believe, why? Because men teach? No, because God teach. His word succeed, influence-you believe.

Word his Lord.

GOSPEL ACCLAMATION

Alleluia

One Father have you, who? God there heaven
One Lord have, who? Jesus Christ.

HOLY GOSPEL ACCORDING TO MATTHEW (23:1–12)

Apostles and people hordes, Jesus inform, "Those scribes and Pharisees, they Moses descend. They your teachers. Everything they tell-you, you obey must; but their actions, follow not. They preach fine-wiggle, but #do-do? Nothing! Suppose there something heavy. Those Pharisees tie-it-up 'Hey, come-here, take-away!', but help refuse. They action something, want people see, applaud. They tend dress ritzy, have (cl:c) band-on-arm, Bible verse inside, plus suppose banquet they go-to, sit special place honor want; temple go-to, sit front want; out street walk, people bow, name-them <u>Rabbi</u> want. You different. Word <u>Rabbi</u> use not. Only-me teacher; you-all learners. Any person here earth name-him father—shh. You have one Father there heaven. Yourself label teacher, not. Myself your teacher. Most important person who? That-one he serve other people. Person boast, God demote-to-baby-finger; but person humble, God promote-to-thumb, praise."

Gospel his Lord.

THIRTY-SECOND SUNDAY IN ORDINARY TIME

BOOK OF WISDOM

(6:12–16)

(Sign wise with left hand throughout) <u>Wisdom</u> (wise) itself beautiful forever. Suppose wise you cherish, easy notice; wise you look-for, find succeed. Suppose wise you want, wise itself influence-you. Time sunrise, you pray-for wise, disappoint not. Receive will you. You wish-for wise, smart you, why? Person wise, worry nothing. Wise itself search++, person worth find, wise give-him, care-for him.

Word his Lord.

RESPONSORIAL PSALM

(63:2, 3–4, 5–6, 7–8)

My soul thirst-for you, Lord, my God.

Yourself my God, I cherish-you / my body hunger, my soul thirst.
Earth dry compare me / feel myself life none, water none.

Your holy place I look-at++ / hope your power, glory see.
Your kindness I cherish more-than life itself / your glory I sign-ASL.

I honor you during my life / my hands sign-ASL, your name summon.
My soul you satisfy compare banquet / I happy, sing praise.

My bed, lie-down, I remember you / all-night I dwell-on you.
Yourself my helper / you protect-me, give-me happy.

FIRST LETTER OF PAUL TO THE THESSALONIANS

(4:13–18)

Brother~sister, we want you understand clear about people themselves finish die—grieve not, hope lose not. We believe Jesus die, resurrect, live again, means what? People die connect-to Jesus, God raise-them live again same-as-him. Inform-you, happen Lord come (cl:1), people dead meet-him (cl:5 lh, 1); my-turn we still live meet-him (cl:5 rh). Lord himself come-down (cl:1), voice loud order, people dead rise will. Finish, we still alive rise-up will together Lord there heaven. From-then-on, with Lord. That story encourage, comfort each-other.

Word his Lord.

GOSPEL ACCLAMATION

Alleluia

Wake-up, ready, why?
Exact day Lord come, you don't-know.

HOLY GOSPEL ACCORDING TO MATTHEW (25:1–13)

Jesus story, "Kingdom his God compare girls ten, they take lantern (cl), go wait-for husband arrive. Five-of-them (l) pea-brain, lantern bring, oil forget, abandon. Five (r) wise, oil bottle bring. Husband postpone++, #ALL fall-asleep. Time midnight, shout! 'Husband here. Come, come!' #ALL ten wake-up, ready lantern. Five pea-brain said, 'Oil, give-me. My fire dissolve.' Five girls wise said, 'No, have enough not. Go store, self buy.' Five-of-them (foolish) away. Wrong, husband arrive. Five-of-them (wise) accompany (cl:5,1) wedding celebrate, door close, lock. Later, five girls come (cl:5), said, 'Open door!' But he answer, 'I don't-know who you.'

Learn what? Pay-attention, ready. Time Jesus come, you don't-know."

Gospel his Lord.

THIRTY-THIRD SUNDAY IN ORDINARY TIME

BOOK OF PROVERBS
(31:10–13, 19–20, 30–31)

Suppose man find wife good, that-one valuable more-than <u>pearl</u>. Husband, he trust her, his heart give-her, love each other whew! Lucky he. She influence good during her life. <u>Wool</u>, <u>flax</u> she buy, cloth make, clothes sew. People poor she help; they need? She give. Suppose woman butter-you-up, maybe deceive (knock). Beauty dissolve will. But suppose woman honor Lord, praise (her). She work++, honor-her. Praise her all-over town.

Word his Lord.

RESPONSORIAL PSALM
(128:1–2, 3, 4–5)

Bless those people, they honor Lord.

You honor Lord, bless you / his way you follow
You work++, succeed / God bless you, cherish you.

Your wife many children born++ / there your home
Your children peace / table sit-around (cl: crooked vv).

Man, himself honor Lord, bless-him / God there heaven bless you
Pray Jerusalem itself succeed / during your life.

FIRST LETTER OF PAUL TO THE THESSALONIANS
(5:1–6)

Exact time Lord come, jot-down, not~need. You know-that Lord will come time you not predict. Happen people laid-back, feel peace, safe; wrong, destroy—compare woman pregnant, wrong, labor. Escape can't (^). You dark, know-nothing, not. You live light, day, understand clear. Dark night we cherish not; well, sleep same other people, not. Continue awake, ready.

Word his Lord.

GOSPEL ACCLAMATION

Alleluia

Lord says, Two-of-us connect continue.
Any person himself connect-to-me, he succeed will.

HOLY GOSPEL ACCORDING TO MATTHEW   (25:14–30)

Jesus story: "Man plan travel. Servants three he summon, money 5,000 give-cash (l); 2,000 give-cash (middle); 1,000 give-cash (r). Finish, go-out. First man, 5,000 invest, increase 5,000 more. Second man same, increase 2,000 more. Third man #do-do? hole dig, money put-in, bury. Long-time-later, man himself come home, servants summon, money what? First man (cl:1) step-forward, bring 5,000 plus 5,000 more. 'Good work. You good servant you; promote-you more important work will I.' Second man (cl:1) step-forward, bring 2,000 plus 2,000 more. 'Smart you. You same good servant. Promote-you more important work will I. Come, happy share.' Last, third man (cl:1) step-forward, said, 'I know you strict, mean man. You tend take++. I afraid, money hide, bury.' 1,000 give-him. (Master) Angry! 'You worthless, you! You know I take++—my money put there #BANK, why not? There tiny-increase interest can. Hey, come-here. Money take-from-him, give-to-him (first man). Person have much, increase will. Person have little-bit, whole-thing lose. This worthless servant, throw-him-out, dark, suffer, cry-out.'"

Gospel his Lord.

CHRIST THE KING

BOOK OF THE PROPHET EZEKIEL

(34:11–12, 15–17)

Lord God says, "My sheep, I myself care-for. Know-that shepherd care-for sheep; suppose scatter, shepherd catch++, gather, care-for—same-as-me my people I care-for. My people compare sheep. Suppose there dark, obscure they scatter, save them will I. I feed them; satisfied, lie-down, rest can they. Suppose lose, I seek, find. Suppose stray, I grab. Suppose hurt, I take-in-arms, wrap-up. Suppose sick, I give heal. Those (other side) fat, strong, destroy will I, but those (sheep) I lead right way. You, my quote 'sheep,' I judge, good, bad separate; sheep, goats, separate."

Word his Lord.

RESPONSORIAL PSALM

(23:1–3a, 3b–4, 5, 6)

Lord, himself my care-er, give-me everything I need.

Lord, he my care-er, give-me everything I need / there grass area, he give me rest;
Near quiet river, he lead me; / my soul he inspire.

Right way he lead-me for his name honor
Suppose dark valley I walk (cl:1), / no-matter, afraid nothing.
He here with-me, accompany, full power, might / courage give-me.

Banquet he prepare, my enemies look-at-me / my head he anoint; my cup (lh) fill-up-overflow.
God good, kind, touch my life / die, I live there his home for ever and ever.

FIRST LETTER OF PAUL TO THE CORINTHIANS (15:20–26, 28)

Christ finish die, resurrect first; later, #ALL dead will same. What cause die? One man, Adam. What cause resurrect? One man, Christ. Follow Adam, #ALL die must, but follow Christ, #ALL live again will; first Christ, later #ALL connect him resurrect will. Finish, every country and power Christ destroy, push-aside; left, kingdom, take-up~give-to God Father. Christ control must until #ALL enemy God defeat—last enemy what? Death itself. Succeed (pah!), son control everything, son will humble, surrender Father, become connected, whole-thing~include.

Word his Lord.

GOSPEL ACCLAMATION

Alleluia

Our ancestor David, his kingdom (sign "his kingdom" near shoulder, putting it in the past) future set-up again, we praise.

HOLY GOSPEL ACCORDING TO MATTHEW (25:31–46)

Jesus inform disciples, "Happen Son of Man come full glory, with angel popular-come-down, I (hon) will sit-throne. #ALL countries hordes face-to-face-me. Group, group I separate; those (r) compare sheep, those (l) compare goats. King tell-them (r) 'Come-here. Father bless-you; come connect heaven. Why? Happen I hungry, you feed-me. I thirsty, water you give-me-cup; friend none, you friendly; I naked, clothes you give-me. Happen I sick, you care-for me; stuck prison, you visit me.' They (r) puzzled, ask, 'Lord, ? food give-you, when? (2) Drink, (3) friendly, (4) clothes give you, (5) visit, when?' King answer, 'Every time you action one-of-these-things (on fingers) for humble brother, same you action for me.' Finish, king tell-them (l), 'Away, you sinners. Go place have fire forever, devil hordes. Why? I hungry, food give-me none; thirsty, drink none; lonely, you

162

friendly none; I naked, clothes give-me none. I sick, prison, you visit me nothing.' They puzzled, 'Lord, ? we see you hungry, thirsty, lonely, naked, sick, prison, and care-for you not, when?' 'Every time brother humble you ignore, same you ignore-me.' Those (l) people #do-do? Forever punish. Those (r) people, forever live."

Gospel his Lord.

PRESENTATION OF THE LORD

BOOK OF MALACHI

(3:1–4)

Lord God say, quote, "See, my informer I send, he prepare way for me." Finish, happen what? Lord, that-one you wait-for up-to-now, he come-down (cl:1), temple touch, new promise bring. Yes, he come near-future.

But day he come, who can tolerate (patient)? He show-up, who brave, who? He compare fire, <u>silver</u> put-in, burn++, pah! Pure, perfect, ready. Priest, he cause-them pure same <u>silver</u>, why? They clean, kill~sacrifice-to Lord can. Now, Jerusalem, its sacrifice God see, satisfied, same long-ago God satisfied.

Word his Lord.

RESPONSORIAL PSALM

(24:7, 8, 9, 10)

King glory, who? Lord himself!

You gates, open-out open-up, / King glory enter
King glory, who? Lord, himself strong, mighty / Lord himself war defeat

You gates, open-out open-up, / King glory enter
King glory, who? Lord, he control heaven / himself King glory.

LETTER TO THE HEBREWS

(2:14–18)

People have body, blood same Jesus have body, blood. Himself willing die, why? Devil destroy; give us free. Now die, we afraid? No!

Angels, Jesus help-them not, but Jew people, he help-them. Means Jesus become full human must. Why? He become same priest-most, faithful, mercy-them, pray-to God please their sin forgive. Jesus himself finish suffer; now people suffer, he understand, help-them can.

Word his Lord.

GOSPEL ACCLAMATION

Alleluia

Light for non-Jews and glory for Jew people.

HOLY GOSPEL ACCORDING TO LUKE   (2:22–40)

Law Moses, Mary, Joseph follow, baby Jesus bring-to Jerusalem, for-for? Offer-to God. Law require what?—every first-born boy offer-to-Lord must. Plus, parents sacrifice birds two must, follow law. Happen there Jerusalem man name Simeon, himself good, holy, he wait-for Messiah arrive. Holy Spirit inform-him what? He live, see Messiah; finish, die. Now, Holy Spirit tell-him temple go-to, see Mary, Joseph, Jesus. He (Simeon) take Jesus (in his arms), praise God, said, "Now die peace can I, why? Your promise satisfied. Savior you send for #ALL people, light for non-Jews and glory for Jew people, I finish see."

Mary, Joseph listen, puzzled. Two-of-them Simeon bless, tell Mary, "This baby will grow-up, cause many people fail and many people succeed all-over Israel. People oppose-him will; and yourself suffer, for-for? People their thought++ show clear can."

There temple have woman prophet name Anna, herself old. Long-ago she married, live with husband 7 years, he die; she live alone up-to-now, now age 84. She frequented temple, all-day, all-night worship, fast, pray. Now arrive, baby see, thank God; finish, she inform-all Jesus save Jerusalem will.

Law obey finish, family group-go #BACK home Nazareth. Baby grow-up, strong, wise; God his grace influence-him.

Gospel his Lord.

Nativity of John the Baptist

BOOK OF THE PROPHET ISAIAH (49:1–6)

#ALL people, far-away, pay-attention-me—Israel speak! Happen I establish not-yet, Lord finish summon-me, my name call-out. Preach tough he give-me, compare sword sharp, but stab not-yet. He tell-me, "You my servant, Israel. My glory you show." Israel work, try, worthless. But God see, he praise will. Lord, himself finish make Israel, for-for? #ALL Jew people summon, come-here Israel, worship Lord. Finish, Israel become glory, strong. Now, Lord tell-me, "You serve God, #ALL Jew people summon, come-here Israel—trivial! I give-you more—now Israel important compare light for #ALL countries, inform-them what? God save-them."

Word his Lord.

RESPONSORIAL PSALM (139:1–3, 13–14, 14–15)

I praise you because you wonderful make me.

Lord, you analyze-me, know me / happen I sit, stand, you notice
My thoughts, you finish know /
Suppose I travel (or) stop, rest, you see / my tendencies (on fingers)
you understand.

You make my body, soul / in my mother pregnant, you make++
I thank you, why? You wonderful make me / everything (out there)
you make wonderful.

My soul you know full / my body you know full same
Secret, you make me / my body you invent, build.

166

ACTS OF THE APOSTLES

(13:22–26)

Paul preach, quote, "Long-ago, God choose <u>David</u> become king, why? <u>David</u> himself good man, obey God. David generations-down, born savior name Jesus. <u>John</u> Baptist, he preach, inform people now life change must. Finish, he tell-them, 'Myself savior, think you? No, not me, but near-future other man come, his shoes touch, I not worth enough.' Means what? You Jew, not-Jew, no-matter. God promise save-you!"

Word his Lord.

GOSPEL ACCLAMATION

Alleluia

People will name-you, quote, "God his prophet."
Why? You travel, preach, prepare for God come-down.

HOLY GOSPEL ACCORDING TO LUKE

(1:57–66, 80)

<u>Elizabeth</u> pregnant, time, born son. Her friends, family happy celebrate. Eight-days later, time for circumcise and name give-him, family think name-him <u>Zechariah</u>, same father. But <u>Elizabeth</u> said, "No. Name <u>John</u>." Understand, family none name <u>John</u>. Family question-to father, <u>Zechariah</u>, baby name-him what? Father talk can't, ask-for paper, write, quote, "Baby name <u>John</u>." Quick, talk again can! He happy, praise God.

Family, friends afraid, gossip spread all-over <u>Judea</u>. People wonder, that baby grow-up, #do-do? Seem God choose-him special. Baby, he grow-up, become strong spirit, live there desert until time begin preach Israel.

Gospel his Lord.

Saints Peter and Paul, Apostles

ACTS OF THE APOSTLES (12:1–11)

Members Christian church, king hate them. <u>James</u>, king order sword-stab. Jews few happy; king see, decide <u>Peter</u> arrest. During celebrate <u>Passover</u>, king order <u>Peter</u> arrest, throw-in jail, soldiers guard. King plan wait <u>Passover</u> finish, <u>Peter</u> bring face-to-face people. <u>Peter</u> stuck jail; Christians pray God protect him. Night before tomorrow court, <u>Peter</u> sleep, chains-on-wrists, soldiers watch-him; wrong happen angel appear, light-shine-from-him. <u>Peter</u>, angel tap-on-shoulder, wake up. Shackles-fall-off-wrists; angel tell-him, "Shoes put-on, belt-put-on; cloak-put-on, follow me." <u>Peter</u> follow, how angel cause happen++, understand not. Seem dream. Two-of-them walk (cl:v) past soldier, arrive gate, itself open. Two-of-them walk (cl:v) narrow street; wrong, angel depart. [<u>Peter</u> now think clear, understand, oh-I-see, angel Lord send for save him. Now king and Jews kill-him can't.]

Word his Lord.

RESPONSORIAL PSALM (34:2–3, 4–5, 6–7, 8–9)

Honor Lord, his angel save-you will.

I honor Lord always / his praise I sign-ASL
My soul have glory with Lord / people humble see, celebrate.

Two-of-us glory give-to Lord / together his name we praise
Past I depend-on Lord, he answer-me / my fear, he remove.

Look-at God, you happy, radiant-face will / you blush, ashamed never
Happen you cry-out-to God, he pay-attention / trouble he save-you

Lord his angel protect you, save you / understand, you honor him
Taste, see, Lord himself good / man trust him (God), he bless.

SECOND LETTER OF PAUL TO TIMOTHY

(4:6–8, 17–18)

I approach time die. I up-to-now stubborn continue; race I finish; faith I cherish. Now crown God have for me. Lord judge me, crown-me—not only me, also #ALL people themselves enthusiastic wait-for him come. Lord up-to-now support-me, give-me strong, I preach gospel country there++, can I. God save me, lion consume-me, he not allow. He continue protect-me until heaven I arrive safe. Glory give-him forever and ever.

Word his Lord.

GOSPEL ACCLAMATION

Alleluia

Your name <u>Peter</u>; this rock, my church I establish
Devil destroy never.

HOLY GOSPEL ACCORDING TO MATTHEW

(16:13–19)

Apostles, Jesus question-to-them, ? "Those people name-me what?" They tell-him, "Some name-you <u>John</u> Baptizer, other name-you <u>Jeremiah</u> or other prophet." (Jesus) "You name-me what?" <u>Simon Peter</u> say, "Yourself true Messiah, son his God." Jesus tell-him, "Bless you, <u>Simon</u>. God himself tell-you true who I (hon). Inform-you, your name <u>Rock</u>; on this rock my church I establish, itself die never. Key for heaven kingdom I give-you. Suppose you decide something bound here earth, there heaven I agree, support. Suppose you decide something free here earth, there heaven I agree free."

Gospel his Lord.

TRANSFIGURATION OF THE LORD

BOOK OF THE PROPHET DANIEL

(7:9–10, 13–14)

I envision see throne; God himself sit there. His clothes white! compare snow; hair white. Throne itself fire, have wheels fire, flame-outward. Many, many people serve him, million people audience. Time meeting, quiet, book open.

Now I see person (l) name son <u>of</u> man, he come (cl:1), face-to-face (God). Control, glory God give-him, become king, he. #ALL people, countries, language serve him (son of man) must. He control forever, break-down never, dissolve never.

Word his Lord.

RESPONSORIAL PSALM

(97:1–2, 5–6, 9)

Lord himself king, whole earth he exceed, control.

Lord himself king, #ALL people celebrate / island there++ happy
Cloud, dark, swirl-around him (cl:1,5) / his throne judge-fair.

Happen Lord look, mountain break-down, / whole earth, Lord control
Heaven announce he judge fair / his glory, #ALL people see.

Lord, yourself control all-over earth / other <u>gods</u>, you exceed.

SECOND LETTER OF PETER

(1:16–19)

We inform-you honest, invent++ nothing. We story Jesus his power; he come-again will, we know-that, how? We finish see God Father give-him glory, announce, quote, "Here my son, I cherish; satisfied me." There holy mountain, voice from heaven we hear. Plus, myself true~work prophet; my inform, you trust can. Better you pay-attention-to-me, follow, compare place dark, candle see, follow. Later, yourself understand.

Word his Lord.

GOSPEL ACCLAMATION

Alleluia

He (hon) my cherish son, satisfy me.
Pay-attention him.

HOLY GOSPEL ACCORDING TO MARK   (9:2–10)

Jesus with <u>Peter</u>, <u>James</u>, and <u>John</u>, four-of them mountain group-go, pray. Jesus pray, wrong, himself change. Face, clothes become white, wow. <u>Elijah</u>, <u>Moses</u>, show-up there (l), there (r), glory, three-of-them discuss Jesus near-future die there Jerusalem. <u>Peter</u>, three-of-them up-to-now sleep, but now wake-up, see those-three glory. <u>Peter</u> tell Jesus, "Lord, three-of-us see you glory, that good. We build tent three, for you++." True, he know-nothing.

Wrong, cloud over. Apostles afraid. They hear voice say, "He (hon) my cherish son. Pay-attention him." Apostles look-around, see Jesus alone. Three-of-them quiet, announce nothing.

Gospel his Lord.

ASSUMPTION OF THE BLESSED VIRGIN MARY

BOOK OF REVELATION

(11:19a, 12:1–6a, 10)

Heaven open, see God his <u>ark</u>. Sky, see woman (center). Herself clothes, sun shine-out-from-her; moon (lh) stand-on; crown, stars, altogether twelve. Woman herself pregnant, cry-out, wring-stomach, ready give-birth. Wrong, show-up (l) what? <u>Dragon</u>, breathe-fire, huge, red, head++ altogether seven, crown++ seven. His <u>tail</u> swish-back-and-forth; stars, swish! 1/3 flutter-to-earth. He stand, wait woman give-birth, plan grab, consume. Woman born son, himself #ALL countries control strict will he. God grab, carry-to throne. Woman escape desert, there God prepare place special for her. Finish, I hear voice loud say: "Now God save succeed, now God control and Jesus muscle succeed."

Word his Lord.

RESPONSORIAL PSALM

(45:20, 11, 12, 16)

Queen there with God, clothes gold.

Queen there with God, clothes gold / gold from where? <u>Ophir</u>

Daughter, pay-attention / your father, your family, push aside.

You beautiful, king cherish you / himself your lord.

Two-of-you full happy, celebrate / king his home enter.

FIRST LETTER OF PAUL TO THE CORINTHIANS

(15:20–26)

Christ finish die, resurrect; himself first person resurrect live again. One man (l) cause #ALL die, now one man (r) cause #ALL resurrect, live again. <u>Adam</u> cause #ALL die; but Christ cause #ALL live again: first Christ himself, later he come again, his followers #ALL resurrect will. Finish, whole power collapse, destroy, dissolve; kingdom left-there, Christ give-to God Father. Christ control continue must until #ALL enemies God destroy. Last enemy what? <u>Death</u>—beat (shot-h).

Word his Lord.

GOSPEL ACCLAMATION

Alleluia

Mary, God take-up, carry heaven
Angels hordes celebrate, happy.

HOLY GOSPEL ACCORDING TO LUKE (1:39–56)

Town there <u>Judah</u> Mary hurry, arrive, house enter, <u>Elizabeth</u> meet, hug. Happen <u>Elizabeth</u>, she hear Mary voice, her baby move. Holy Spirit inspire (Elizabeth), she cry-out: "Bless you, most high woman! Bless your baby pregnant! Mother his Lord visit me, why? Myself trivial, me. Instant your voice I hear, my baby happy, move. Bless you, why? Lord his promise you trust."

Mary said, "My heart announce Lord himself wonderful; my spirit happy celebrate God, my savior, why? He notice-me (hon), his servant humble. #ALL people future name-me holy. God himself mighty, wonderful things he finish action for me; his name true holy. He mercy continue++ for people—understand, they honor him. His power he show, how? People proud, feel themselves wise, he mess-up. People power, throne, he throw-out; people humble, poor, he put-there (in their place). People hungry, he give-them satisfy, but people rich, he give-them nothing, send-away. He up-to-now support Israel; always he mercy++, same he promise our ancestor Abraham, pass-down++ forever."

Mary stay with <u>Elizabeth</u> three-months; finish, #BACK home.

Gospel his Lord.

EXALTATION OF THE HOLY CROSS

BOOK OF NUMBERS (21:4–9)

Israel people travel++, patient-suffer, complain Moses, quote, "Awful you lead-us from Egypt here desert die, why? Food, water, none. Food here, we hate!" Those people, Lord punish, how? Send snake many, bite++, cause die. People tell Moses, "We complain, sorry. We sin. Please you pray God snakes remove." Moses pray for people, Lord tell-him, "Yourself make pole (cl:f,f), smake metal put-on-top, stab-in-ground. Any person snake bite, he look (at pole), healed will he." Moses make snake <u>bronze</u>, pole put-on-top, stab-in-ground. Happen snake bite, person look (at pole), healed succeed.

Word his Lord.

RESPONSORIAL PSALM (78:1–2, 34–35, 36–37, 38)

Lord his actions, forget not!

People, pay-attention my teach / my talk, please listen!
Story I tell-you / secret honest, I explain will.

Happen God kill-them, they quick sorry / want follow God again.
They remember, oh-I-see, God true our support / himself expert save us.

They butter-up (God), they slick-talk / they promise these things (on fingers) but lie.
Their heart cherish God not / they faithful obey him not.

But God himself full mercy, their sin he forgive / he destroy-them not.
His anger he restrain / he lose-temper not, calm-down.

LETTER OF PAUL TO PHILIPPIANS (2:6–11)

Christ Jesus, himself true God, yes, but he cherish it (point upward) not. No, Jesus willing born same slave. Himself human 100%. He humble obey Father, accept die there cross. Now, God raise-him live again, give-him name #ALL other name exceed. Happen Jesus name hear, every person kneel-down must, there heaven, here earth, there hell, every voice announce, give glory God Father, quote, "Jesus Christ true Lord."

Word his Lord.

GOSPEL ACCLAMATION

Alleluia

Christ, we adore, praise you.
Cross you die, world save.

HOLY GOSPEL ACCORDING TO JOHN (3:13–17)

Nicodemus, Jesus tell-him, "Who finish see heaven? None—sh! Myself finish touch heaven. Long-ago desert, Moses snake lift-up (cl:s,s), same must myself lift-me-up, they look-at-me, believe, live forever. Yes, God love world so-much, his only Son he give, for-for? Any person believe Son, that person die not; he live forever. Son God send for world punish? No. World save through Son, God want."

Gospel his Lord.

BOOK OF REVELATION

(7:2–4, 9–14)

Myself, <u>John</u>, I see angel, east, come (cl:1), God his <u>seal</u> (fs and sign) hold. There angels four, they have power land and sea ruin can. Angel, he shout, "Destroy land, sea, trees, suspend; first servants his God seal (cl:f on forehead)." Seal++ altogether how many? 144,000 from every Israel group++. Finish, I see people hordes, count impossible, every country, color skin, language, hordes. They stand face-to-face throne, there Jesus (name <u>Lamb</u>). #ALL have clothes white, leaf <u>palm</u> they hold. They cry-out, "Save comes from God, himself sit there throne, and from Jesus." #ALL (1) angels, (2) leaders, (3) four living things, #ALL kneel++, worship God, say, "Amen (in palm)! Praise, glory, wise, thanks, honor, power, strong give-to our God forever and ever, Amen!" One leader question-me, "Those people white clothes—who? From where?" I answer, "You know. I don't-know." He tell-me, "Those people stubborn~continue, no-matter awful trouble, suffer. Their clothes they wash in blood from him <u>lamb</u>—now white, clean."

Word his Lord.

RESPONSORIAL PSALM

(24:1–2, 3–4, 5–6)

Lord, we your people, your face wish see.

Lord control earth whole / #ALL people he control
Earth, he establish it / ocean, river, he make.

Lord his mountain, who climb, who? / his holy place stand, who?
That-one sin none, heart pure / worthless things, he want never.

That-one, Lord bless-him will / God save-him
Same #ALL people they obey God / his face they search-for.

FIRST LETTER OF JOHN

(3:1–3)

Father love us, wow! He name-us his children. We his children true~work. But people here world understand not—why? Jesus they don't-know. Cherish friend, we true God his children now; but future, what? Know-nothing. We know-that happen Jesus come (cl:1) again, we become same-as-him. See himself (hon) will we. Every person, suppose future see Christ hope, keep themselves pure continue, same-as Christ, himself pure.

Word his Lord.

GOSPEL ACCLAMATION

Alleluia

Lord says, You work++, tired, come-here
Rest, I give-you.

HOLY GOSPEL ACCORDING TO MATTHEW

(5:1–12)

Jesus see people hordes, mountain walk-up (cl:v-legs), sit, disciples sit-around-him (cl:crooked 4,4). Jesus teach, "You people depend-on God, bless you, why? Kingdom heaven he give-you will. You people sad, grief, bless you—God kind-to-you. You people humble, bless you—land take-up control will. You hunger, thirst for judge~fair, bless you—satisfy will. You mercy-out, bless you—God mercy-you. Your heart cherish God, bless you—see God will you. You bring peace, bless you—name-you children his God. You live right; wrong hit suffer, persecute-you, bless you, why? Future you, heaven, connect. Suppose you follow me, wrong happen people insult-you, hate-you lie~gossip about you, bless you. Celebrate happy! Why? There heaven have wonderful <u>reward</u> gift."

Gospel his Lord.

DEDICATION OF THE LATERAN BASILICA

BOOK OF THE PROPHET EZEKIEL (47:1–2, 8–9, 12)

There temple, angel carry-me. Door, I see water flow-toward-me, east (toward me)—temple front, east (toward me). Water flow-to-left, south. Angel lead-me (r) north gate, out, come-around-to-front (cl:1,1). Water I see flow-to-left. Angel tell-me, quote, "That water flow where? Ocean, flow-into. Ocean, its water salt, water flow-into, become clean, <u>fresh</u>, salt dissolve. River flow, cause grow++ animal, plant, fish, various. Flow, ocean enter, become clean. Trees, fruit, grow plenty. Leaves green, fruit delicious, sour never. Every-month, new fruit, why? Temple water flow. Fruit eat, delicious; leaves, make medicine."

Word his Lord.

RESPONSORIAL PSALM (46:2–3, 5–6, 8–9)

God his city have water~river, happy; God himself live there.

God himself give-me protect, mighty / time-period trouble, he help-me
Earth messed-up, no matter, we afraid not / mountain break-down, no-matter.

Have river, itself cause God city happy / God himself live there
City, God there middle / time sunrise, God help-it.

Lord himself here with us / God himself defend us
Come-here! God his actions see / wonderful things he action here earth.

SECOND LETTER OF PAUL TO THE CORINTHIANS (3:9c–11, 16–17)

Brother~sister, you-all compare house. God teach-me, help-me build wise. First, foundation (base) I establish, flat (cl:b,b). Other people build there. Understand, build careful must, why? Have foundation only-one, that-one Jesus Christ. Other place build, worthless.

?? Know-that yourself God his temple? His Holy Spirit live in you. Suppose temple, person destroy, God see, destroy-him. Why? Temple holy, means yourself holy.

Word his Lord.

GOSPEL ACCLAMATION

Alleluia

This house I choose, bless.
Live there forever, will I.

HOLY GOSPEL ACCORDING TO JOHN (2:13–22)

Jew <u>Passover</u> near-future, near, Jerusalem Jesus go-to. Temple arrive, people see, they #do-do? Cow, sheep, bird sell; other people sit, money budget share. Jesus make same <u>whip</u>, string, crack-whip, tables overturn, money coins roll-away. Jesus bawl-out, "Away! My Father house, you change sell place. Finish!" Apostles remember Bible predict, quote "Your house I enthused cherish"—oh-I-see. Jew people question, "Your authority action all-this, where? Proof where?" Jesus answer, "This (hon) temple destroy, 3 days later I set-up again." (Jews) "This temple build require 46 years, but you 3-days set up? Sick you!" True, Jesus mean what temple? His body. Later, Jesus die, resurrect finish, apostles remember, look-back Jesus story, oh-I-see, believe.

Gospel his Lord.

GLOSSARY OF SIGNS

Away-they-go	Natural "shooing" motion, one or both hands, bent B handshape, palms down, sweep to palm-forward in the direction of the shooing
Beginning-to-end	Left hand open 5, palm in, right hand B handshape, palm left
Between-the-eyes	Left hand in front of body, palm facing in; fingers pointing up and slightly parted; right hand index suddenly stabs through the space between left index and middle finger (be sure to separate fingers before stabbing!)
Big-brains	Cup handshape on both hands, placed at forehead one in front of the other
Can't (^)	As the index finger crooks into an X, it turns sharply inward
Cl	Classifier; use hands to show shape and usage of named item
Cover-up	Left 5 hand palm up, right 5 hand palm down; right moves backward over left, as if smoothing something over
Dash	Left hand flat, palm down, right hand flat, palm up; right palm brushes against left palm as right moves up and outward toward right
Exchange-words	Open hands, palms up, move alternately back and forth between the two people who are exchanging words
Fine-wiggle	Fine, thumb against chest, fingers wiggle
Frequented	Left hand 1 handshape; right hand B handshape, palm in, fingers pointing to left hand 1; fingertips of B repeatedly move toward left 1 in circular motion; may actually touch
Fuss-back-and-forth	Thumbs and fingertips of both hands tap against each other while both hands move back and forth between the two people who are fussing
Good-riddance	Both hands palm out directionally, quickly close to flat-O's
Gotcha	U handshape moves in quick movement toward person who is being "got"
Grief	Heart-wring
Gulp	Throat-clutch—oops!
Hands-off	Middle finger of open 8 hands brush something off both shoulders
Hey!	Wave hand up and down, as if getting someone's attention
Hm	Thoughtful gesture, rubbing chin
Holier-than-thou	Both hands at shoulders, palms out, fingers pointing up, ring fingers bent down at knuckle
Immerse	The "dunking" sign for baptism
Isaiah	Sign "prophet" using I handshape
Jump-at-chance	Right hand from C to S, snatches something off left palm
Kick-back	Crooked index fingers on both hands fall apart, representing legs hanging over the arms of an easy chair
Knock	Left hand 1 handshape, right hand knocks sharply on side of index finger
Know-nothing	O or F handshape bounces gently in front of forehead

Know-that	B hand at forehead, index touching forehead, bends sharply forward at wrist
Laid-back	"Casual"; both 5 hands, palms down, move together from left to right to left in relaxed manner
Learn-lesson	Fingertips of flat-O touch forehead, then hand opens and fingers slap forehead
Let's-see	See-see
Little-story	"Story" signed with small double movement, "narrate"
Look-like	Face-same
Make-me-sick	Right hand only signs "sick" but twists as it touches forehead
Mooch	Both hands in "duck" handshape, right hand "bites" left, draws it toward self
More-than	The sign for "than"
Mull-over	Thumb and fingertips tap quickly and lightly together while whole hand moves in a very small circle in front of forehead
Next-to-her	Make "agent" sign (both flat hands, palms facing each other, move down slightly), them move both hands purposefully to the side and sign it again
No-wave	Both 5-hands, palms forward, shake back and forth
(on fingers)	left 5-hand, palm-in, right index points to fingertips
Pah!	Succeed, signed once, strongly
Phooey	Right hand palm forward swishes to palm-down in a natural gesture of dismissal
Promiscuity	left hand 5, right hand bent-V sweeps across ends of left fingers
Pull-in-head	Left hand C like cup; right hand S like a head; left C encircles right forearm, right arm moves down quickly, like a turtle pulling in its head
Put-him-there	S handshape, like grabbing a staff, movement directional
Recruit	Left hand 1 handshape; right hand bent-V hooks left 1 and draws it toward self
Ritzy	3 handshape, fingers pointing up, thumb bumps up against chin
Same-as	Y handshape, palms forward, moves back and forth from left to right or between the things that are the same
Same-same	1 handshape on both hands, palms down; sides of index fingers touch, separate, move slightly to the right, and touch again
Same-around	Both hands Y handshape, palms down, thumbs almost touching; circle hands in wide horizontal arc
See-if	See-see
Set-up	Opposite of "collapse"; fingers lift to a tent-shape
Shot-h	S handshape moves forward directionally and ends with sudden change to H handshape

So-what	Right hand, bent-B, palm in, backs of fingers under chin; hand flips forward and opens to palm in, fingers pointing straight up
Stand-strong	Looks like "tree" except right hand is a fist
That's-all	Finish! Ending with hands at shoulders, palms forward
Tool-around	Open-8 hands, one pointing up, the other pointing down, circle in a series of horizontal loops
Trivial	"Nothing-to-it"; two F hands, palms out, shake horizontally
Un-popular	Left hand 1; right hand 5 moves backward, away from the 1
Up-to-now	Same as "since," but bigger and slower
Well . . .	Natural gesture, both hands open in front of body, palms up
Whoa!	Claw handshape, palm in, moves back and forth in front of face
Whole-thing	The sign for "all"